AI WEIWEI ARCHITECTURE

EDITED BY CAROLINE KLEIN

Introduction 4

"Make it simple!" The multisided figure is a curator, manager of an art gallery, promoter of artists and publisher. As an artist he has been a central player in Chinese avant-garde from its very beginnings in the early 80's. Ai Weiwei acts in China as one of the most dedicated political activists and web blogger who is committed to human rights and freedom of speech. Since his participation in the documenta in 2007, he belongs to the best known representatives for regime-critical art from China or better to say for artistic regime criticism. In 1999 the artist decided to direct his talent also toward architecture for the simple reason that he did not want to rely on architects in China. In 2003 the autodidact founded his studio FAKE Design in order to manage his growing architectural work. The rapid, inconsiderate modernization in China and the dealing with the tradition always form the subtext of his artistic and architectural works. Ai Weiwei translates the notion of traditional construction into a contemporary idiom. He does not attempt to emulate the architectural style of a bygone era. Inspired by the context, common places like villages or the local people, he adapts his buildings to basic techniques and to the know-how of local craftsmen, questions notions of authenticity, originality and simplicity. In answer to building codes that require new structures to blend into the already existing fabric, Ai Weiwei bases his modest, minimalist approach on the most affordable solutions. In contrast to the glass-and-steel high-rises going up in China, his constructions are nearly always built of gray brick. The easily available and very durable material reveals an aesthetic, reached by limited means and symbolizes for him the essential qualities of architecture. His buildings take their power from material texture, human scale, stunning proportions and – as the interior and exterior spaces are equally treated – quiet and peaceful open spaces. Simple volumes of bare geometry create enclosed courtyards and labyrinthine passages with an introverted, contemplative atmosphere. His projects aim for social interaction and for an ideal for living in a country where runaway economic development has shown little regard for the everyday life of the individual. More than a final product, he considers architecture as an ongoing, endless system. For Ai Weiwei, architecture is not just a repository for daily activity but above all an opportunity to improve quality of life and to further its inhabitants' possibilities. Just as he took by chance the opportunity to create buildings, he could all at a sudden decide to interrupt this architectural phase. We are very excited to discover more of his buildings!

„Einfachheit!" Ai Weiwei ist äußerst vielseitig: Er kuratiert Ausstellungen, leitet eine Kunstgalerie, fördert Künstler und ist Herausgeber. Als Künstler stellt er eine zentrale Figur in der chinesischen avant-garde seit ihrer Anfänge in den frühen 80'er Jahren dar. Er wirkt in China als einer der engagiertesten Politaktivisten und *web blogger*, der sich für Menschenrechte und Redefreiheit einsetzt. Seit seiner Teilnahme an der documenta 2007 zählt er zu den bekanntesten Repräsentanten für regimekritische Kunst aus China beziehungsweise für künstlerische Regimekritik. 1999 kam Ai Weiwei aus dem einfachen Grund zur Architektur, weil er den Baukünstlern im Land nicht traute. 2003 gründete der Autodidakt das Studio FAKE Design, um die wachsende Zahl seiner Projekte zu bewältigen. Die unterschwellige, intendierte Botschaft seiner Kunstwerke und der Architektur ist stets die rasante, rücksichtslose Modernisierung in China und der Umgang mit der Tradition. Ai Weiwei übersetzt den Begriff der traditionellen Konstruktion auf zeitgenössische Art, ohne mit dem architektonischen Stil eines vergangenen Zeitalters wetteifern zu wollen. Der Entwurf inspiriert sich am Kontext, an Dörfern oder der einheimischen Bevölkerung, passt sich an grundlegende überlieferte Bautechniken und das *know-how* der örtlichen Handwerker an und wirft die Frage der Begriffe von Echtheit, Originalität und Einfachheit auf. Als Antwort auf Bauvorschriften, die von neuen Strukturen verlangen, mit bereits vorhandenen zu verschmelzen, stützt Ai Weiwei seine bescheidene, minimalistische Annäherung auf erschwingliche Lösungen. Im Gegensatz zu den Stahl- und Glashochhäusern, die in China hochgezogen werden, bestehen seine Bauten fast immer aus grauem Ziegel. Das leicht verfügbare und äußerst haltbare Material weist eine mit einfachen Mitteln realisierte Ästhetik und die für ihn wesentlichen architektonischen Qualitäten auf. Textur, menschlicher Maßstab, überwältigende Proportionen und ruhige und friedliche Außenräume machen die Stärke seiner Bauten aus. Innen- und Außenräume werden gleichwertig behandelt. Einfache geometrische Körper erzeugen introvertierte, kontemplative Innenhöfe und labyrinthische Durchgänge. Seine Projekte zielen auf soziale Wechselwirkung und ein Lebensideal für ein Land, in dem die davonrennende Wirtschaftsentwicklung kaum Rücksicht auf den individuellen Alltag nimmt. Ai Weiwei betrachtet Architektur nicht als ein endgültiges, fertiges Produkt, sondern als einen andauernden Vorgang. Anstatt nur ein Behältnis für die täglichen Aktivitäten zu sein, dient ein Gebäude vor allem zur Verbesserung der Lebensbedingungen und bietet den Bewohnern Gelegenheit für künftige Veränderungen. So zufällig er mit dem Bauen begann, so unvermittelt könnte er die architektonische Schaffensphase auch wieder beenden. Warten wir also gespannt auf weitere Bauten seiner Handschrift!

"¡Diciéndolo sencillamente!" La figura multifacética es la de un curador, gerente de una galería, promotor de artistas y editor. Desde sus inicios, a principios de los años 80, ha sido un personaje central del avant-gard chino. Ai Weiwei actúa en su país como uno de los más dedicados activistas políticos y *web blogger*, involucrado con los derechos humanos y la libertad de expresión. Desde su participación en documenta en 2007, pertenece a los más conocidos representantes del arte de la crítica al régimen chino, o mejor dicho, de la crítica artística al régimen. En 1999, el artista decidió dirigir su talento hacia la arquitectura, por la sencilla razón de que no confiaba en los arquitectos de su país. En 2003, el autodidacta fundó su estudio FAKE Design para gerenciar su creciente trabajo arquitectónico. La modernización rápida y desconsiderada en China, así como la presencia de la tradición, siempre conforman el subtexto de sus trabajos artísticos y arquitectónicos. Ai Weiwei traduce la noción de construcción tradicional a un lenguaje contemporáneo. No intenta emular el estilo arquitectónico de tiempos pasados. Sus proyectos se inspiran en el contexto, así como en los pueblos o la población local, adaptando las técnicas básicas y el *know-how* de artesanos locales a nociones de autenticidad, originalidad y simplicidad. Como respuesta a los códigos de construcción, que requieren las nuevas estructuras se mezclen en la trama existente, Ai Weiwei sustenta su acercamiento, humilde y minimalista, en la economía de sus soluciones. En contraste fuerte para las torres de cristal y acero que erigen en China, sus edificaciones están casi siempre construidas con ladrillo gris. Este material, muy duradero y fácilmente disponible revela una estética, construida con medios muy limitados y simboliza para él las cualidades esenciales de la arquitectura. Su diseño elemental adquiere su fuerza de la textura, la escala humana, las proporciones impactantes y los espacios abiertos tranquilos y apacibles. Los espacios interiores como los exteriores son igualmente tratados. Volúmenes simples de geometría desnuda crean patios delimitados y pasajes laberínticos con una atmósfera contemplativa e introvertida. Sus edificios claman por la integración social y un ideal para vivir en un país donde el desarrollo económico desenfrenado ha mostrado poco respeto a la vida del individuo. Más que un producto final, considera la arquitectura como un interminable sistema en evolución. Para Ai Weiwei la arquitectura no constituye solamente un contenedor para la actividad diaria sino, sobre todo, una oportunidad para mejorar la calidad de vida y las posibilidades futuras de los habitantes. Así como él asumió por casualidad la posibilidad de crear edificios pudo, de repente, terminar con su fase arquitectónica. ¡Hoy en día miramos hacia delante, esperando ver elaboraciones futuras de su puño y letra!

« Que de la simplicité ! » La personalité multifacette est un conservateur, directeur d'une galerie, promoteur d'artistes et rédacteur. Comme artiste Ai Weiwei jouait un rôle central dès le commencement de l'avant-garde chinois, au début des années 80. Il agit en Chine, entant que activiste politique et *web blogger*, parmi les plus engagés, qui se consacre aux droits de l'homme et à la liberté d'expression. Depuis sa participation à documenta en 2007, il appartient aux représentants les plus connus pour l'art critique du régime chinois ou mieux pour la critique artistique du régime. En 1999 il a décidé de diriger son talent également vers l'architecture pour la simple raison qu'il n'avait pas confiance en les architectes de son pays. En 2003 l'autodidacte a fondé son bureau FAKE Design afin de contrôler son travail architectural grandissant. La modernisation rapide, inconsidérée en Chine et le respect de la tradition constituent le sous-texte de ses travaux artistiques et architecturaux. Ai Weiwei traduit la notion de construction traditionnelle dans un idiome contemporain, toutefois sans essayer d'imiter le style architectural d'une ère passée. Inspirés par le contexte, les villages ou les autochtones, ses projets s'adaptent aux techniques basiques et au savoir-faire d'artisans locaux, et posent les questions d'authenticité, originalité et simplicité. Dans la réponse aux règlements du bâtiment qui exigent des nouvelles structures de se fondre dans le tissu déjà existant, Ai Weiwei base son approche modeste et minimale sur les solutions les plus abordables. En contraste avec les hauts tours de verre et d'acier érigés en Chine, ses bâtiments sont presque toujours construits de brique grise. Le matériau facilement disponible et très durable révèle qu'une esthétique, faite avec des moyens limités, symbolise pour lui les qualités essentielles de l'architecture. Ses bâtiments gagnent ses forces de la texture, de l'échelle humaine, des proportions sensationnels et – comme les espaces intérieurs et extérieurs sont également traités – des espaces ouverts tranquilles et paisibles. Des volumes simples et géométriques créent des cours fermées et des passages labyrinthiques, procurant une atmosphère introvertie, méditative. Ses bâtiments visent l'interaction sociale et un idéal pour vivre dans un pays où le développement économique galopante a montré peu d'égard pour la vie de l'individu. Plus qu'un produit fini, il considère l'architecture comme un processus en cours, sans fin. Pour Ai Weiwei, un bâtiment ne représente pas seulement un contenant pour l'activité quotidienne, mais surtout une occasion afin d'améliorer la qualité de la vie et de rendre service aux habitants. Ainsi, tout comme il a saisi par hasard l'occasion de créer des bâtiments, il pourrait tout à coup décider de terminer cette phase de création architecturale. Nous attendons donc avec intérêt de nouvelles constructions de son esprit !

"**Semplice!**" Ai Weiwei presenta una personalità polivalente e complessa: opera infatti come curatore museale, responsabile di una galleria d'arte, promotore di artisti ed editore. Da artista ha svolto un ruolo centrale nell' avanguardia cinese fin dalle sue origini nei primi anni 80. In Cina milita tra gli attivisti politici e *web blogger* più impegnati nel campo dei diritti umani e la libertà di parola. Sin dalla sua partecipazione alla documenta nel 2007, risulta fra i rappresentanti più noti per l'arte regime-critica cinese ovvero per la critica artistica del regime. Nel 1999 ha deciso di dirigere il suo talento anche verso l'architettura per la semplice ragione che non si fidava degli architetti del suo paese. Nel 2003 l'autodidatta ha fondato il suo studio FAKE Design per poter gestire i progetti architettonici ormai in aumento. La modernizzazione rapida e tumultuosa in Cina come pure il porsi alle tradizioni, costituiscono sempre il tema in filigrana delle sue opere artistiche e architettoniche. Ai Weiwei traduce il concetto di costruzione tradizionale in un linguaggio contemporaneo, senza cercare di emulare lo stile architettonico di un'epoca trascorsa. Ispirati dal contesto, dai villaggi o la gente del posto, i suoi progetti si adattano alle tecniche di base e al *know-how* degli artigiani locali e si interrogano sui concetti di autenticità, originalità e semplicità. Per ottemperare alle norme edilizie che impongono alle nuove strutture di fondersi con quelle esistenti, Ai Weiwei basa il suo approccio umile e minimalista sulle soluzioni più economiche. In contrasto con i palazzoni di vetro e acciaio che sorgono in Cina, le sue costruzioni sono quasi sempre in mattone grigio. Il materiale facilmente disponibile e molto resistente rivela un'estetica, ottenuta tramite mezzi limitati e incorpora, secondo lui, le qualità essenziali dell'architettura. I suoi edifici traggono forza dalla texture, dalla misura umana, da proporzioni sensazionali e – perché l'interno ed esterno hanno la medesima importanza – da spazi aperti calmi e pacifici. Volumi semplici e geometrici creano cortili chiusi e passaggi labirintici con un'atmosfera introversa, contemplativa. I progetti mirano a un'interazione sociale, come alla vita ideale in un paese dove lo sviluppo economico galoppante ha mostrato poco riguardo per l'esistenza dell'individuo. Più che un prodotto finale, Ai Weiwei considera l'architettura un processo continuo e infinito. Un edificio non rappresenta solo un deposito per le attività quotidiane ma soprattutto un'opportunità per migliorare la qualità della vita e per fornire agli abitanti future possibilità. Così come ha colto casualmente l'occasione di creare edifici, potrebbe decidere all'improvviso di interrompere questa fase architettonica. Aspettiamo quindi con ansia altri edifici della sua firma!

"**开始吧！**" 艾未未的多面性堪称极致：策划展览，管理画廊，资助艺术家，出版人。80年代初期中国先锋艺术兴起，从那时起他一直是代表人物。在中国他是最热心致力于维护人权和言论自由的政治活动家，他的博客在因特网上非常有名。自从2007年参加了文献展以后他是批评集权的艺术或者说艺术地批评集权最著名的代表人物。1999年艾未未走向建筑，只缘于他不能信任那些建筑艺术家。2003年，为了完成不断增多的项目，没学过建筑的他成立了FAKE建筑设计室。
中国现代化发展之迅猛和无所顾忌，以及对待传统的态度往往成为艾未未建筑和艺术作品的潜台词。他无意与昔日建筑风格相争，而是将传统的建筑方法转变为当代艺术。他的设计灵感源于环境，村落，神秘的居民，他的设计尽可能地适应基本的传统建筑技术和当地建筑工人的知识水平，并提出了真实、原创和简练的问题。面对建筑法规对新建筑的规定，对现有的东西进行整合，保证了他的极简主义的解决方案。与中国钢筋和玻璃结构的高层建筑相反，他的建筑差不多永远使用的是青砖。这种容易购买并且特别耐用的材料表明了一种必要的、用一种简单的方法即可以实现的美学，对他来说这是一种更重要的建筑质量。内在结构，人的准则，使人倾倒的比例，安静和平的外部空间，强化了他的自然设计的力度。建筑内部和它的外部环境拥有同样的价值。简单的几何体幻化出内倾和沉思的庭院以及迷宫般的通道。他的作品指向社会的相互作用和生活的理想，在这个国度里，迅猛的经济发展几乎不再顾及个体。艾未未认为建筑不是一件最终的、完成了的产品，而是一个连续的发生过程。艾未未的建筑，不是人们日常活动的场所，而是提高生活条件并给居住在里面的人提供一种未来变化的机会。他在如此的偶然中走向建筑，自然也会突然终止他的建筑创作。所以，我们满怀紧张地期待着他的新作。

PROJECTS

AI WEIWEI STUDIO
STUDIO AND RESIDENCE
CAOCHANGDI, BEIJING, CHINA
Design date: 06.1999
Construction date: 06 – 10.1999
Total built area: 500 m²

The artist Ai Weiwei launched his career as an architect with the design of his own studio house. A wall encloses a courtyard whose northern width is spanned by the building that is constructed with red bricks and poured-in-place concrete with a facade made up of Beijing's traditional blue-gray bricks. Inside, the red bricks, partly painted white, fill the exposed, reinforced concrete frame. Skylights flood the two story-high atelier and exhibition space. The reception room's window is the only aperture in the otherwise closed-front wall facing the courtyard. The open internal structure preserves exciting visual axes from various points. The rough detailing and the witty application of vernacular material have become Ai Weiwei's trademark in Caochangdi, a district recently transformed into Beijing's new hub of cultural production.

Der Künstler Ai Weiwei wandte sich mit dem Bau seines eigenen Atelier-Wohnhauses erstmals der Architektur zu. Eine Mauer umgrenzt den Innenhof, dessen nördliche Breite vom Gebäude komplett eingenommen wird. Es besteht aus einer innen sichtbaren und mit roten Ziegeln ausgemauerten Stahlbetonkonstruktion, deren Außenwände mit den regionaltypischen blaugrauen Ziegeln versehen sind. Die Innenwände sind zum Teil weiß verputzt und Oberlichter versorgen den zweigeschossigen Atelier- und Ausstellungsraum mit Tageslicht. Im Empfangsbereich bietet ein Fenster die einzige Öffnung zum Innenhof in der ansonsten geschlossenen Fassade. Die offene Raumstruktur schafft spannende Ein- und Ausblicke zwischen den einzelnen Bereichen. Die grobe Detaillierung und die geistreiche Anwendung des einheimischen Materials wurden zu Ai Weiweis Markenzeichen in Caochangdi, das in Pekings neuen kulturellen Mittelpunkt umgestaltet wurde.

El artista Ai Weiwei ha iniciado su carrera como arquitecto con su propia casa-estudio. Un muro encierra un patio cuya extensión hacia el norte està ocupada por la construcción que está hecha de ladrillo rojo y de hormigón vaciado en sitio, con la fachada realizada con los tradicionales ladrillos gris-azulados de Pekín. En el interior el ladrillo rojo, pintado en parte de blanco, rellena la estructura de hormigón armado. Los tragaluces inundan de luz el taller de doble altura y el espacio expositivo. La ventana de la habitación de la entrada constituye la única abertura en la fachada frente al patio, que sin ella se hallaría completamente cerrada. La estructura abierta en el interior asegura juegos visuales apasionantes desde diferentes ángulos. El detalle basto y el empleo del material vernacular se ha convertido en la marca de fábrica de Ai Weiwei en Caochangdi, hoy transformado en el nuevo centro de producción cultural de Pekín.

C'est en commençant par dessiner sa propre maison-atelier que l'artiste Ai Weiwei a entrepris son métier d'architecte. Un mur entoure une cour dont la largeur au nord est traversée par le bâtiment, construit en briques rouges et en ciment coulé sur place dont la façade est réalisée avec les traditionnelles briques gris-bleu de Pékin. À l'intérieur, les briques rouges, partiellement peintes de blanc, remplissent la structure renforcée en béton apparent. Les lucarnes inondent de lumière la double hauteur de l'atelier et la surface d'exposition. La fenêtre de l'entrée est la seule ouverture de la façade face à la cour qui, autrement serait totalement fermée. La structure interne ouverte garantit la présence d'axes visuels interessants de plusieurs points de vue. Le détail brut et l'utilisation géniale du matériau vernaculaire sont devenus la marque de fabrique de Ai Weiwei dans le quartier Caochangdi, qui aujourd'hui représente le nouveau centre de production culturelle de Pékin.

L'artista Ai Weiwei ha iniziato la sua carriera di architetto con il progetto della propria casa-studio. Un muro racchiude un cortile la cui ampiezza a nord è completamente occupata dall'edificio in mattoni rossi e cemento colato sul posto che presenta una facciata nel tradizionale mattone grigio-blu di Pechino. All'interno, il mattone rosso, in parte dipinto di bianco, riempie il telaio di cemento armato. I lucernari inondano di luce la doppia altezza dell'atelier e lo spazio espositivo. La finestra della sala d'ingresso costituisce l'unica apertura nella facciata di fronte al cortile, altrimenti completamente chiusa. La struttura interna aperta offre interessanti assi visivi da differenti angolazioni. Il grezzo dettaglio e l'astuta applicazione del materiale vernacolare è diventato il marchio di Ai Weiwei nel quartiere Caochangdi, oggi trasformato nel nuovo centro di produzione culturale di Pechino.

"工作室" 艺术家艾未未以自己的工作室与住房为起点，开始了建筑师生涯。一堵墙围起了一处院子。院子北面是住房与工作室。建筑材料是红砖，在恰到好处的位置填入了混凝土结构。正面用北京传统的蓝灰砖砌成。建筑内部部分涂成白色，露出的部分则用红砖填充，这也强化了混凝土结构。而两倍高度的工作室与展览室都充满了来自顶灯的光线。接待室的窗户是正对庭院的唯一窗口，否则房屋的正面就是完全封闭的。开放的内部结构保留了激动人心的多角度视觉轴。

CONCRETE

LANDSCAPE DESIGN | BEIJING, CHINA
Design date: 05 - 06.2000
Construction date: 06.2000 - 09.2001
Size: 11.6 m x 4.2 m

The fountain project is located in the heart of Beijing's earliest SOHO development. Surrounded by six 28 story buildings, the almost cylindrical form is the source for a fountain from which water trickles through beautiful masonry work to an adjacent basin. The massive concrete sculpture and the cascading basin create an attraction within the high rise neighborhood.

Der Brunnen liegt im Herzen von Pekings erstem SOHO Projekt und ist von sechs 28-stöckigen Gebäuden umgeben. Die Quelle entspringt in der fast zylindrischen Form, von der das Wasser durch schöne Mauerwerkkonstruktionen in ein angrenzendes Becken geleitet wird. Die massive Betonskulptur und das abfallende Bassin erzeugen eine Anziehungskraft innerhalb der Hochhausnachbarschaft.

El proyecto de la fuente se sitúa en el corazón del desarrollo de la primera SOHO en Pekín. Rodeada de seis edificios de 28 pisos, la forma casi cilíndrica es el origen de una fuente de agua orientada a una cuenca adyacente a través de un valioso trabajo de mampostería. La escultura de hormigón macizo y la cuenca con cascada constituyen una atracción en el barrio de los edificios multipisos.

Le projet de la Fontaine se situe à Pekin, au cœur de la première SOHO. Entourée par six palais à 28 étages, la fontaine a une source à la forme presque cylindrique qui dirige l'eau vers un bassin adjacent par un murage digne d'estime. La sculpture en béton massif et le bassin à cascade constituent une attraction à l'intérieur d'un quartier aux bâtiments multi-étages.

Il progetto della Fontana è situato a Pechino nel cuore della prima SOHO. Circondata da sei palazzi di ventotto piani, la forma quasi cilindrica è la sorgente di una fontana d'acqua che direziona l'acqua, attraverso un pregevole lavoro di muratura, verso un bacino adiacente. La scultura in calcestruzzo massiccio e il bacino a cascata creano un'attrazione all'interno del quartiere dagli edifici multipiano.

"混凝土" 喷泉项目的位置在北京最早的小型或家庭办公室开发区的中心。喷泉的水源外形接近于圆柱形，周围是6座28层的建筑。水流经过漂亮的石材作品，流进附近的一个水池。大量的混凝土雕刻以及瀑布池吸引了周围高层建筑物里的人们。

IN BETWEEN
INSTALLATION | BEIJING, CHINA
Design date: 05 – 06.2000
Construction date: 06 – 09.2001
Size: 3.5 m x 3.5 m x 3.5 m

"In Between" bridges the gap between art and architecture. Individual components come together to achieve a cogent physical structure and to enjoy a symbiotic relationship with space. The archetypal house-shape intersects the floor. In addition to the intersection, the blue painted structure is tilted at an angle. The skewed and apparently severed form playfully raises the question of alternatives.

„In Between" schließt die Lücke zwischen Kunst und Architektur. Individuelle Bestandteile treffen aufeinander, um eine stichhaltige, physische Struktur zu erreichen und eine symbiotische Beziehung mit dem Raum einzugehen. Die archetypische Hausform zerschneidet den Fußboden, scheint, in ihm zu versinken. Zusätzlich zur Kreuzung kippt das blaue Volumen an einer Ecke. Die schiefe und scheinbar durchtrennte Form bringt spielerisch die Frage nach Alternativen auf.

"In Between" salva la distancia entre arte y arquitectura. Componentes sencillos se unen para conseguir una estructura física acogedora y agradar con una relación simbiótica con el espacio. El arquetipo con forma de casa atraviesa el pavimento. Además de esta intersección, la estructura pintada de azul, está inclinada en ángulo. La forma oblicua y aparentemente quebrada plantea, juguetonamente, una alternativa.

« In Between » comble la lacune entre l'art et l'architecture. Des éléments individuels se mêlent pour camper une structure physique coactive et jouir d'une symbiose avec l'espace. La forme archétypique de la maison coupe le sol. Outre cette intersection, la masse, peinte de bleu, est inclinée à angle. La forme oblique et apparemment brisée pose plaisamment la question d'une alternative.

"In Between" colma il divario tra arte e architettura. Singoli componenti si uniscono per dar vita ad una struttura fisica cogente e godere di una relazione simbiotica con lo spazio. L'archetipica forma di casa interseca il pavimento. Oltre a questa intersezione, la massa, dipinta di blu, è inclinata ad un angolo. La forma obliqua e apparentemente spezzata pone scherzosamente il quesito di alternative.

"在中间" 联接了艺术与建筑的差距。把不同的成分组合成为令人赞叹的自然结构并与空间达成共生的关系。房屋原型与地面产生交叉。除了这种交叉，喷涂成蓝色的建筑主体倾斜一定角度。这种倾斜和它明显分离的外型诙谐地提出了一个二选一命题。

BAR JIA 55
BEIJING, CHINA
Design date: 2001
Construction date: 04 – 06.2001
Total floor area: 300 m²

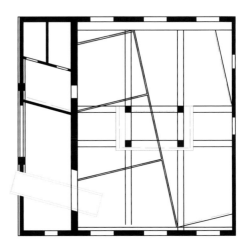

The fast changing urban lifestyle in Chinese cities is epitomized by the interior design of locations like restaurants and bars. The original site for Bar Jia 55 was a square space with a low ceiling and four concrete columns located in the center. By using a single material, laminated light gray fiberboard, to resurface and redesign both wall and ceiling, a feeling of upside down icebergs or glacial cracks has been created. This is reinforced by the use of ceiling lighting.

Der sich rasant ändernde Lebensstil in chinesischen Städten verkörpert sich besonders in der Innenraumgestaltung von Restaurants und Bars. Die Ausgangssituation der Bar Jia 55 war ein Raum mit einer niedrigen Decke und vier, im Zentrum gelegenen Betonsäulen. Als einziges Material kamen hellgrau laminierte Holzfaserplatten zum Einsatz, um eine neue Oberfläche zu erzeugen, sowohl Wand als auch Decke neu zu entwerfen und somit ein Gefühl von umgestürzten Eisbergen oder Eisspalten hervorzurufen, dass durch die Deckenbeleuchtung verstärkt wird.

La vida urbana de las ciudades chinas, en continuo cambio, representada mediante el diseño interior de bares y restaurantes. La forma ya existente para Bar Jia 55 era un espacio cuadrado con un techo bajo y cuatro columnas de hormigón situadas en el centro. Utilizando un único material - ligeras planchas laminadas de fibra de madera gris - para recubrir y rediseñar de nuevo tanto las paredes como el techo, ha sido creada la sensación de iceberg bocabajo o grietas en el hielo, sensación reforzada por la iluminación del techo.

Le changement rapide de la vie urbaine en Chine se reflète dans la réalisation des intérieurs de cafés et restaurants. L'espace préexistant pour Bar Jia 55 était une surface carrée au plafond surbaissé avec quatre colonnes en béton au milieu. Grâce à l'emploi d'un seul type de matériau pour recouvrir et redessiner les murs aussi bien que le plafond, les plaques légères laminées en fibre de bois grise, on a crée l'impression d'icebergs renversés ou crevasses de glace, une sensation renforcée à l'aide d'un éclairage au plafond.

Il rapido cambiamento della vita urbana cinese si riflette nel design degli interni di bar e ristoranti. Lo spazio preesistente per Bar Jia 55 consisteva in una superficie quadrata con un soffitto basso e quattro colonne di calcestruzzo poste al centro. Con l'utilizzo di un unico materiale, leggere placche laminate in fibra di legno grigio, allo scopo di ricoprire e ridisegnare sia la muratura che il soffitto, si crea l'impressione di iceberg capovolti o di crepacci di ghiaccio, una sensazione rafforzata dalla realizzazione di un'illuminazione a soffitto.

"甲55酒吧"目前是一块正方形区域，天花板很低，中间立着四根混凝土圆柱。使用同一种材料即水泥板的目的是为了墙和天花板的重新铺设以及重新设计。这样创造出一种类似冰山上下颠倒的或者冰川裂缝的感觉，并通过顶灯光线的运用而得到加强。

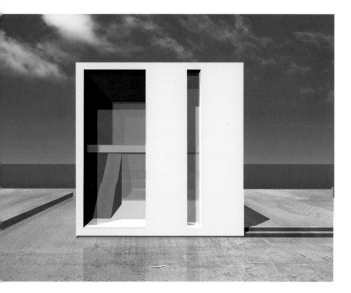
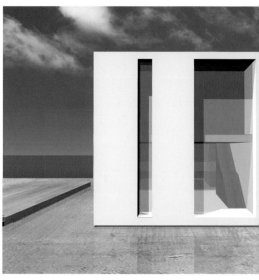
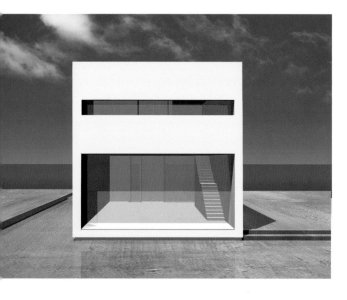
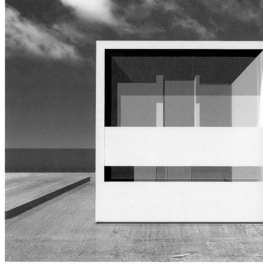

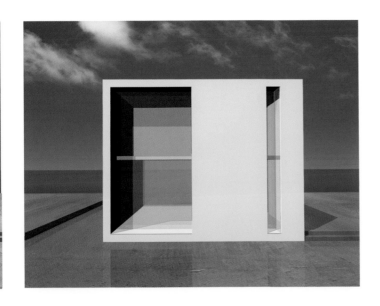

BOAO VILLA
RESIDENTIAL BUILDING
HAINAN, CHINA
Unrealized
Design date: 2001

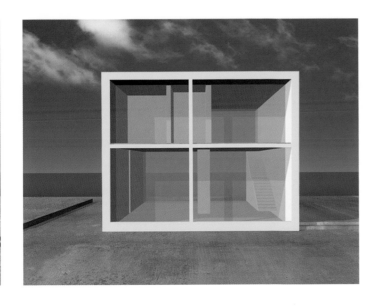

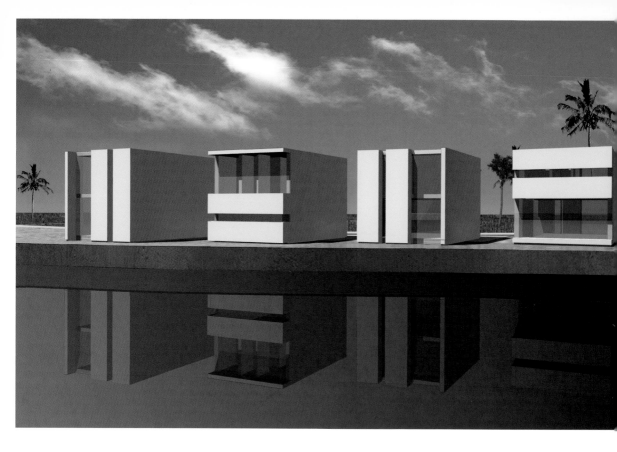

The approach used for the villa design was to create a single cube typology that when rotated and adjusted, would become four sub typologies. Each villa is equal in dimension and varies only in the articulation of their window areas and location. The four types A, B, C, and D are arrayed between the access road and the water, and are laid out as independent cubes or as conglomerated structures.

Beim Entwurf der Villa ging es darum, eine einzelne Kubus-Typologie zu entwickeln, die, gedreht und justiert, wiederum vier Untertypologien erzeugt. Die Villen sind gleich groß, nur die Fensteranordnung und -position variiert. Die vier Arten A, B, C, und D liegen zwischen der Zufahrtstraße und dem Wasser und sind als unabhängige Würfel oder Konglomerate angelegt.

El concepto del proyecto Boao Villa fue en crear una tipología cúbica sencilla que, girada y adaptada, crease cuatro subtipologías. Todas las casas de campo tienen las mismas dimensiones y se diferencian sólo en la articulación y colocación de las ventanas. Los cuatro tipos: A, B, C y D, están alineados entre la calle de acceso y el agua y están colocadas bien como cubos independientes o como conglomerados.

Le projet de la maison consista en la création d'une seule typologie cubique qui, tournée et ajustée de façon secondaire, puisse créer quatre sous-typologies. Toutes les maisons ont les mêmes dimensions et ne se différencient que pour l'articulation et la position des fenêtres. Les quatre typologies, A, B, C et D, se trouvent entre la voie d'accès et l'eau et se présentent comme des cubes indépendants aussi bien qu'agglomérés.

Il progetto della villa prevede la creazione di una singola tipologia cubica che, ruotata e adattata, potesse generare quattro sotto-tipologie. Tutte le ville hanno la stessa dimensione e variano soltanto nell'articolazione e nella disposizione delle finestre. Le quattro tipologie, A, B, C e D, sono schierate tra la strada di accesso e l'acqua e disposte come cubi indipendenti o agglomerati.

"博鳌别墅"　　别墅化设计的目的在于创造单一的立体形态，加以旋转或调整时可以产生另外4种形态。每一间别墅的尺寸相等，只是在窗户大小与位置的结合方面有所区别。四种类型分别为A型，B型，C型和D型，被安排在通道和水源之间，布局为独立的个体或集合体。

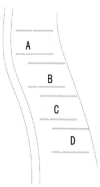

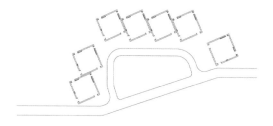

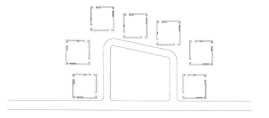

YIWU RIVER BANK
LANDSCAPE DESIGN
JINHUA, ZHEJIANG, CHINA
Design date: 04 – 06.2002
Construction date: 06.2002 – 06.2003
Total site area: 1.595.000 m²

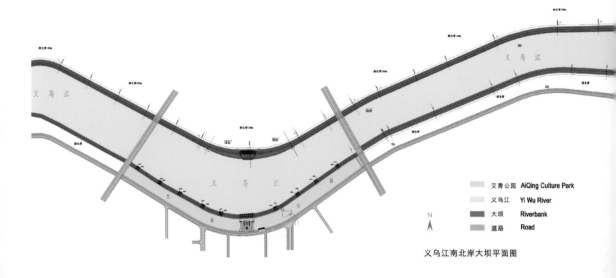

义乌江南北岸大坝平面图

	艾青公园	AiQing Culture Park
	义乌江	Yi Wu River
	大坝	Riverbank
	道路	Road

In order to connect the river with the town Ai Weiwei designed a 85-meter-wide and 1.600-meter-long green belt as well as the embankment. The riverside was converted from a technical building into a publicly accessible promenade and thus, achieved urbane character and high quality. A central square intermediates between river and town and is covered by a grid of stone columns whose heights steadily rise. This stele group is surrounded by water which runs off about steps to the river. Triangular sculptures of natural stone integrated into a big stair arrangement create the transition of the square to the river. The stringent composition and the simple monochrome materials generate a homogeneous, strong appearance, highly aesthetic and functional spaces. The combined effect of the dam and the park resumes the traditional relationship between man and water, making the river an active part of the city by activating the neglected waterfront and thus, enriching people's lives with its river environment while providing opportunities for river and water development in the future.

Ai Weiwei gestaltete den Übergang zwischen Fluss und Stadt in Form eines 85 Meter breiten und 1.600 Meter langen Parks, wie auch die Uferbefestigung. Das Flussufer wurde von einem technischen Bauwerk für den Überschwemmungsfall in eine öffentlich zugängliche Promenade umgewandelt und gewann so urbanen Charakter und hohe Aufenthaltsqualität. Ein zentraler Platz vermittelt zwischen Fluß und Stadt und wurde mit einem Raster aus Steinsäulen angelegt, deren Höhen gleichmäßig ansteigen. Die Stelengruppe ist von Wasser umgeben, welches über Stufen zum Fluss abläuft. Den Übergang vom Platz zum Fluss prägen dreieckige Natursteinskulpturen, die in eine große Treppenanlage eingebunden sind. Die stringente Gesamtkomposition und die einfache, monochrome Materialität erzeugen ein homogenes, starkes Erscheinungsbild und ästhetische und funktionale Räume. Die Kombination aus Damm und Park greift die traditionelle Beziehung zwischen Mensch und Wasser wieder auf, integriert den Fluss aktiv in die Stadt, indem das vernachlässigte Ufer wiederbelebt und so das Leben der Bevölkerung bereichert wird. Gleichzeitig bieten sich unzählige Gelegenheiten für künftige Fluss- und Wasserplanungen.

Con la finalidad de unir el río con la ciudad, Ai Weiwei diseñó un cinturón verde de 85 metros de ancho y 1.600 metros de longitud, así como la colocación de unos terraplenes. La orilla del río fue transformada de una construcción técnica para contrarrestar posibles inundaciones en un paseo de acceso público y adquirió, por tanto, carácter urbano y alta calidad. Una plaza central actúa como punto intermedio entre el río y la ciudad y está ocupada por una retícula de columnas de piedra cuya altura aumenta constantemente. Este grupo de estelas está rodeado por agua que fluye por los escalones hacia el río. Esculturas triangulares de piedra natural, integradas en un gran sistema de escaleras, crean el paisaje entre la plaza y el río. La composición rigurosa y los materiales sencillos y monócromos crean una fuerte homogeneidad y revelan espacios muy estéticos y funcionales. El efecto combinado del terraplén y del parque sintetizan la relación natural entre el hombre y el agua, haciendo del río parte activa de la ciudad, reactivando el paseo fluvial abandonado y enriqueciendo por tanto la vida de los habitantes con el entorno de su río y ofreciendo a la vez nuevas oportunidades de desarrollo futuro para el agua y para el propio río.

Afin de relier le fleuve à la ville, Ai Weiwei réalisa une ceinture verte de 85 mètres de largeur et 1.600 mètres de longueur et s'occupe de la réalisation des digues. La rive du fleuve fut transformée d'une structure technique pour éventuelles inondations en promenade publique et gagna donc un caractère urbain et de haute qualité. Une place centrale fait fonction de point intermédiaire entre fleuve et ville et est occupée par une grille de colonnes en pierre dont la hauteur augmente constamment. Ce groupe de stèles est entouré par l'eau qui s'écoule des marches vers le fleuve. Des sculptures triangulaires en pierre naturelle, intégrées dans un grand système d'escaliers, créent le passage entre place et fleuve. La composition rigoureuse et les matériaux simples et monochromes confèrent une forte homogénéité et révèlent des espaces hautement esthétiques et fonctionnels. L'effet combiné du barrage et du parc est une synthèse de la relation naturelle entre homme et eau, à travers laquelle le fleuve devient une partie active de la ville et réveille le quai négligé en enrichissant donc la vie des habitants avec l'environnement de leur fleuve et en offrant en même temps de nouvelles opportunités de développement futur pour l'eau et le fleuve même.

Allo scopo di collegare il fiume alla città, Ai Weiwei progettò una cintura verde, larga 85 e lunga 1.600 metri, oltre alla sistemazione degli argini. La riva del fiume fu trasformata da una costruzione tecnica per contrastare gli eventuali allagamenti, in una passeggiata di pubblico accesso e guadagnò, pertanto, carattere urbano e d'alta qualità. Una piazza centrale funge da punto intermedio fra fiume e città ed è occupata da una griglia di colonne in pietra la cui altezza aumenta costantemente. Questo gruppo di stele è circondato dall'acqua che scorre via su gradini verso il fiume. Sculture triangolari in pietra naturale, integrate in un grande scalinata, creano il passaggio fra la piazza ed il fiume. La composizione rigorosa ed i materiali semplici e monocromi conferiscono al progetto una forte omogeneità e rivelano spazi altamente estetici e funzionali. L'effetto combinato dell'argine e del parco sintetizza la naturale relazione tra l'uomo e l'acqua, rendendo il fiume parte attiva della città, riattivando il lungofiume trascurato e arricchendo di conseguenza la vita degli abitanti con l'ambiente del loro fiume, e dando nel contempo nuove opportunità di futuro sviluppo per l'acqua e per il fiume stesso.

"义乌河岸" 为了将义乌河与城市连接起来，艾未未设计了85米宽，1600米长的绿化带与河堤。在公共散步区为防备洪水而修建的技术性建筑使河岸发生变化，提高了宜居质量。处在河流与城市之间的中央广场布满石柱群，高度规则地上升。环绕石柱群的流水从台阶上流向河流。自然石块被雕刻成三角形，组成大型的阶梯式布局，从而完成从广场到义乌河的过渡。紧凑的内容与颜色简单的用料创造出相似而坚固的外形以及具有高度审美观与功能性的区域。公园与堤坝的综合效果继承了人与水的传统关系，通过开发受到忽视的河滨地区，使河流成为城市活跃的一部分，丰富了人们的生活，同时也为河与水未来的开发提供了条件。

AI QING CULTURAL PARK
LANDSCAPE DESIGN
JINHUA, ZHEJIANG, CHINA
Design date: 03 – 07.2002
Construction date: 06.2002 – 03.2003
Total site area: 122.000 m²

The Park is located on a 122.000 m² terrain, with a maximum length of 1.600 meters. The theme for the sculpture of the park is "Song of Light", a poem written by Ai Weiwei's father Ai Qing, perhaps the best-known poet of his generation and among the most acclaimed Chinese literary figures of the 20th century who was exiled to western China. The famous poet was born in Jinhua, and the Ai Qing Cultural Park with its massive masonry pillars commemorates him and his poems.

Der Park liegt auf einem 122.000 m² großen Gebiet und erstreckt sich über eine Länge von 1.600 Metern. Das Thema der Parkskulptur ist „Lied des Lichts", Titel eines Gedichts von Ai Weiwei's Vater, dem in Jinhua geborenen Ai Qing, einer der bekanntesten Dichter seiner Generation und unter den gefeiertsten chinesischen Literaten des 20. Jahrhunderts, der nach Westchina ins Exil verbannt wurde. Der Ai Qing Cultural Park erinnert mit seinen massiven Mauerwerksäulen an ihn und seine Gedichte.

El parque se ubica en un terreno de 122.000 m², con una longitud máxima lateral de 1.600 metros. El tema de la escultura del parque es "Canción de luz", título de una poesía del padre de Ai Weiwei, Ai Qing, nacido en Jinhua; quizás el más famoso poeta de su generación y entre los personajes literarios chinos más aclamados del siglo XX, y exiliado en China occidental. Ai Qing Cultural Park con sus imponentes pilares de mampostería, está dedicado a su memoria y a sus poemas.

Le parc occupe une surface de 122.000 m² et a une largeur maximale de 1.600 mètres. Le thème de la sculpture qui se trouve à son intérieur, « Chanson de lumière », est le titre d'un poème écrit par le père de Ai Weiwei, Ai Qing, né à Jinhua, qui est peut-être le poète le plus célèbre de sa génération et une des figures littéraires les plus acclamées du XXème siècle, exilé dans la Chine occidentale. Avec ses imposantes colonnes maçonnées, Ai Qing Cultural Park est dédié à sa mémoire et à ses œuvres.

Il parco si trova su un terreno di 122.000 m², la cui massima lunghezza è di 1.600 metri. Il tema della scultura nel parco, "Canzone di luce", è il titolo di una poesia del padre di Ai Weiwei, Ai Qing, forse il più rinomato poeta della sua generazione e tra le figure letterarie cinesi più acclamate del ventesimo secolo, nato a Jinhua ed esiliato nella Cina Occidentale. Ai Qing Cultural Park con le sue imponenti colonne in muratura, è dedicato alla sua memoria e alle sue opere.

"艾青文化公园" 这座公园占地122,000 平方米，最大长度达1,600米。公园内的雕塑主题为"光明之歌"，该命名源于艾未未的父亲——艾青的一首诗，他也许是那个时代最为著名的诗人，是中国二十世纪最受尊敬的文化名人之一，被流放到中国西部。这位著名的诗人出生于金华，"艾青文化公园"的大型石柱就是为了记念诗人与他的诗篇。

AI QING MIDDLE SCHOOL
LANDSCAPE DESIGN
JINHUA, ZHEJIANG, CHINA
Design date: 2003
Construction date: 2004
Total area: 31.429 m²

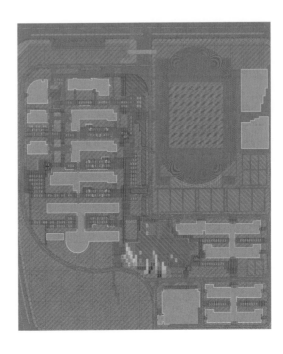

The landscape design for the Ai Qing Middle School began after the completion of the schools overall plan and thus became a revision to a pre-existing site. The site slopes gradually from north to south with a total elevation change of seven meters. The redesigned master plan relocated the academic buildings in order to focus the design more on the open spaces. A grid was implemented to design the landscape, creating zones for relaxation, reading, sports, meeting points and for assemblies.

Das Landschaftsdesign für die Ai Qing Grundschule begann nach der Vollendung des Gesamtplans der Schulen und wurde so zu einer Revision der vorhandenen Bedingung. Das Gelände fällt nach und nach von Nord nach Süd ab und weist insgesamt einen Höhenunterschied von sieben Metern auf. Der Master Plan fügte die Schulgebäude neu im Gelände ein, um den Schwerpunkt auf die Außenräume zu setzen. Ein Raster gliedert die Landschaft und schafft Zonen zur Entspannung, zum Lesen, für Sport, Treffpunkte und Versammlungen.

El diseño del paisaje de la escuela media Ai Qing comenzó después de terminarse el proyecto general de la escuela y por lo tanto se convirtió en la revisión del lugar preexistente. El lugar tiene una pendiente gradual de norte a sur con un desnivel global de siete metros. El plan maestro rediseñado reubicaba los edificios académicos con la finalidad de focalizar mejor el diseño de los espacios abiertos. Se ha diseñado de nuevo el paisaje implementando un reticulado, creando así zonas para el relax, la lectura, los deportes, los lugares de encuentro y de reunión.

Le projet de paysage de l'école élémentaire Ai Qing commença après la conclusion du projet général de l'école et se présente donc comme la révision d'une situation déjà existante. Le site déscend graduellement du nord au sud avec un dénivellement de sept mètres. Grâce au nouveau plan d'ensemble, les bâtiments académiques ont été repositionnés en se focalisant d'avantage sur les espaces ouverts. A travers l'insertion d'une grille, le paysage est été organisé en zones pour la relaxation, la lecture, les sports, les rencontres et les réunions.

La progettazione del paesaggio della scuola media Ai Qing iniziò dopo il completamento del progetto generale della scuola e si propone pertanto come la revisione di una preesistente situazione. Il sito scivola gradatamente da nord a sud con un dislivello totale di sette metri. Grazie al nuovo piano generale, gli edifici accademici sono stati riposizionati focalizzandosi maggiormente sugli spazi esterni. Un reticolato articola il paesaggio, creando zone per il relax, la lettura, gli sport, luoghi di incontro e di riunione.

"艾青中学" 艾青中学的风景区在学校的整体规划完成后开始设计。因此这项设计便成为对原来的区域进行改造。整个区域从北至南缓慢下降形成斜坡,整体落差达到7米。重新设计的总体规划对教学楼的位置进行调整,从而重点设计开放区域。设计风景区时使用了网格,划分出休闲区,读书区,运动区,集合点以及集会区。

SONGSHAN LAKE
CULTURE AND EXHIBITION CENTER
DONGGUAN, GUANGDONG, CHINA
Unrealized
Design date: 05 – 08.2003
Total floor area: 9.540 m²
Building area: 2.016 m²

Ai Weiwei was in charge of the project's overall plan, whereas the design of the four programmed buildings – an exhibition center, a multimedia center, a restaurant and an experimental theater – were divided between him and three other architects. The ensemble of buildings creates a multifunctional area that is linked by and enclosed by the looping pedestrian circuit designed by Ai Weiwei. The exhibition center serves as a platform for public art and industrial product design. It is composed of four identical rectilinear volumes, each rotated 90° from the structure below. The different orientation of each structure is supported by a group of glazed platforms which provide panoramic views to diverse directions and consequently enables natural light to penetrate the exhibition spaces.

Ai Weiwei war für die Projektplanung verantwortlich, wohingegen die vier vorgesehenen Gebäude – ein Ausstellungs-, ein Multimediazentrum, ein Restaurant und ein experimentelles Theater – zwischen ihm und drei weiteren Architekten aufgeteilt wurden. Das Gebäudeensemble erzeugt ein multifunktionales Zentrum, das durch einen, von Ai Weiwei entworfenen, schleifenförmigen Fußgängerstrom verbunden und umschlossen ist. Das Ausstellungszentrum dient als Plattform für öffentliche Kunst und Industriedesign. Es besteht aus vier identischen, geradlinigen Bauten, die sich um 90° vom unteren Volumen drehen. Die unterschiedliche Ausrichtung der Körper wird durch gläserne Plattformen unterstützt, die verschiedenartige Ausblicke und natürlichen Lichteinfall in den Ausstellungsflächen ermöglichen.

A Ai Weiwei se le encargó planificar el plan general del proyecto mientras los cuatro edificios previstos - un centro de exposiciones, un centro multimedial, un restaurante y un teatro experimental - fueron subdivididos entre él y otros tres arquitectos. El conjunto forma un área multifuncional unida y encerrada por un circuito peatonal diseñado por Ai Weiwei. El centro de exposiciones, formado por cuatro construcciones rectilíneas idénticas que giran 90° respecto a la construcción subyacente, actúa como plataforma para los productos de diseño industrial y obras artísticas. La orientación diferente de cada construcción está apoyada en un grupo de plataformas vidriadas que ofrece panorámicas visuales diferentes, permitiendo además a la luz natural penetrar en los espacios expositivos.

Ai Weiwei fut chargé de planifier le projet alors que les quatre bâtiments prévus – un centre sportif, un centre multimédia, un restaurant et un théâtre expérimental – furent partagés entre lui et trois autres architectes. L'ensemble des bâtiments forme une zone multifonctionnelle reliée et entourée par un circuit pour piétons projeté par Ai Weiwei. Le centre d'exposition, composé par quatre bâtiments rectilignes identiques qui tournent de 90° par rapport au bâtiment sous-jacent, sert de plateforme pour le design de produits industriels et les œuvres artistiques. L'orientation différente de chaque bâtiment est supportée par un groupe de plateformes en verre qui fournit des vues panoramiques différentes, en permettant, en plus, à la lumière naturelle de pénétrer dans les espaces d'exposition.

Ai Weiwei fu incaricato di pianificare il progetto mentre i quattro edifici previsti - un centro espositivo, un centro multimediale, un ristorante ed un teatro sperimentale - furono suddivisi tra lui ed altri tre architetti. L'insieme degli edifici crea un'area multifunzionale, collegata e racchiusa da un circuito pedonale progettato da Ai Weiwei. Il centro espositivo, composto da quattro identiche costruzioni rettilinee che ruotano di 90° rispetto alla costruzione sottostante, funge da piattaforma per i prodotti di design industriale e opere d'arte. Il diverso orientamento di ogni costruzione è supportato da un gruppo di piattaforme di vetro che fornisce differenti visuali panoramiche, permettendo inoltre alla luce naturale di penetrare gli spazi espositivi.

"松山湖文化展览中心" 艾未未负责这项工程的总体规划，计划内的四座建筑——展览中心，多媒体中心，餐厅以及实验剧场——被分配给他和其它三位建筑师。建筑团队设计的多功能区，是通过由艾未未设计的环形步行通道连接并环绕起来。展览中心可视为公共艺术以及工业产品设计的展览平台。展览中心由位置处于一条线上的四间相同展厅组成，每间展厅都与下一间成９０度角。每间展厅的方向不同，由一组玻璃平台支撑，提供了各个方向的全景视角，使得自然光可以进入展览区。

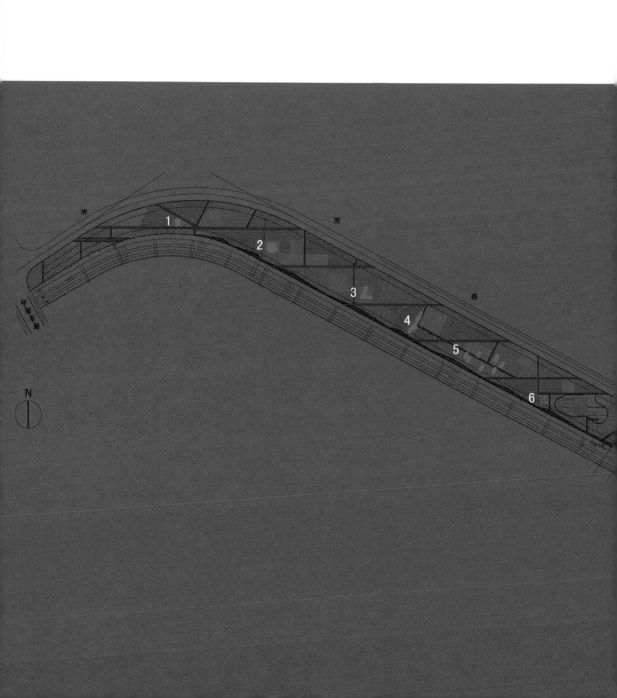

JINHUA ARCHITECTURAL ART PARK
LANDSCAPE DESIGN, MASTER PLAN
JINHUA, ZHEJIANG, CHINA
Design date: 04.2004 – 09.2005
Construction date: 02.2005 – 10.2007
Total site area: 176.000 m²

The Jindong government's proposal to design a park and a small museum for ancient pottery on the north bank of the Yiwu River resulted in the invitation of architects from all over the world to build an architectural park with seventeen mini public structures. Ai Weiwei was in charge of the master plan and the landscape design. Apart from the specific program for each pavilion and the request to use local materials and for costs to be reasonable, there were no other restrictions in the brief. Up until now, Chinese parks are mostly functional and monotonous, serving to improve bad air and for the rejuvenation of the population. This park is a collection of small structures with a humanitarian objective: It not only offers a wide range of activities but also sharpens the senses. A cultural park which should sensitize to the built environment.

Der Vorschlag der Jindong Regierung, einen Park und ein kleines Museum für antikes Porzellan auf der Nordseite des Yiwu Flusses zu entwerfen, führte zu der Idee, Architekten aus aller Welt einzuladen, einen architektonischen Park mit siebzehn öffentlichen Ministrukturen zu bauen. Ai Weiwei war für den Master Plan und das Landschaftsdesign verantwortlich. Abgesehen von der spezifischen Pavillonfunktion und der Bitte, lokale kostengünstige Materialien zu verwenden, gab es keinerlei Vorgabenbeschränkung. Bislang sind Grünräume in China meist funktional und monoton, sie dienen zur Verbesserung der schlechten Luft und zur Regeneration der Bevölkerung. Dieser Park verfolgt ein humanitäres Ziel: Mit seiner Ansammlung von kleinen Strukturen bietet er eine Vielzahl von Betätigungen und schärft die Sinne. Ein Kulturpark, der für die gebaute Umwelt sensibilisieren soll.

A raíz de la propuesta del gobierno de Jindong de diseñar un parque y un pequeño museo de antiguos objetos de cerámica en la orilla norte del río Yiwu, arquitectos de todo el mundo fueron invitados a realizar un parque arquitectónico con diecisiete pequeñas estructuras públicas. A Ai Weiwei se le encargó el proyecto piloto y el diseño del paisaje. Aparte del plan específico para cada pabellón y la petición de emplear materiales locales con razonables costes, no se puso ninguna restricción. El parque recoge pequeñas estructuras con fines humanitarios. Los parques chinos siempre han sido casi todos funcionales y monótonos, entendidos como áreas para mejorar la calidad del aire y fortalecer a los ciudadanos. En cambio, este parque ofrece una amplia gama de actividades y desarrolla la percepción de todos los sentidos. Un parque cultural que debería sensibilizar al entorno construido.

Après la proposition du gouvernement de Jindong de réaliser le parc et un petit musée de poteries antiques le long de la rive nord du fleuve Yiwu, des architectes du monde entier furent invités à réaliser un parc architectonique avec dix-sept petites structures publiques. On attribua à Ai Weiwei le projet pilote et le design du paysage. Au delà du programme spécifique pour chaque pavillon et la prétention d'utiliser des matériaux locaux avec des coûts raisonnables, on n'imposa aucune autre restriction. Jusqu'à ce moment là, la majorité des parcs chinois était fonctionnelle et monotone, ils étaient interprétés comme des lieux pour améliorer la qualité de l'air et où la population peut se ressourcer. Ce parc avec sa collection de petites structures à but humanitaire : il offre une vaste gamme d'activités et développe la perception de tous les sens. C'est un parc culturel qui devrait sensibiliser les gens aux constructions environnantes.

Come conseguenza della proposta del governo di Jindong di progettare un parco ed un piccolo museo di antichi oggetti di ceramica sulla riva nord del fiume Yiwu, architetti da tutto il mondo furono invitati a realizzare un parco architettonico con diciasette piccole strutture pubbliche. Ad Ai Weiwei fu assegnato l'incarico del progetto pilota e del design del paesaggio. A parte il programma specifico per ogni padiglione e la richiesta di utilizzare materiali locali con ragionevoli costi, non fu posta alcuna restrizione. I parchi cinesi sono sempre stati per la maggior parte funzionali e monotoni, intesi come aree atte alla purificazione dell'aria e dove far ritemprare la popolazione. Questo parco invece con la raccolta di piccole strutture segue uno scopo umanitario: offre una vasta gamma di attività e sviluppa la percezione di tutti i sensi. Un parco culturale che dovrebbe sensibilizzare all'ambiente edificato circostante.

"金华建筑艺术公园" 金东区政府的最初提案是设计一座公园以及一座小型博物馆，展览义乌河北岸的古代陶器，这项提案后来演变成邀请世界各地的建筑师建造一座建筑艺术公园，包含17座小型公共建筑。艾未未负责总体方案以及风景区设计。除了每个展览厅的详细规划，以及使用当地材料和控制成本的要求，设计简报里就没有其它限制了。公园内的小型建筑群是以人文主义为主旨。迄今为止，中国的公园大多只具有　　　　　　功能性目的且设计单调，用来改善空气及有利于人口再生。这座公园通过它的许多小型建筑设施为人们提供了进行多种多样活动的可能性，　　　锻炼人的感知能力。文化公园应该使人感知周围的环境。

chweizer

Emanuel Christ, Christoph Gantenbein

Tatiana Bilbao

Liu Jiakun

Wang Xingwei, Xu Tiantian

nner Bruendler Architects

Ding Yi, Chen Shuyu

Wang Shu

eiwei

Toshiko Mori

Erhard An He Kinzelbach

Design Consulta

Fernando Romero

Herzog & de Meuron

nael Maltzan

Yung Ho Chang

51

NEOLITHIC POTTERY MUSEUM
JINHUA, ZHEJIANG, CHINA
Design date: 05 – 10.2004
Construction date: 02.2005 – 10.2007
Total built area: 336 m²

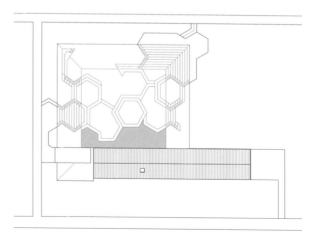

One of the seventeen pavilions of the Jinhua Architectural Park is designed by Ai Weiwei, a museum for ancient Chinese pottery. Playing with tradition and abstraction, the design derives from the vernacular house shape with walls and a gabled roof. Due to its hexagonal form in cross section, the building is highly recognizable. It subtly fits into the landscape. Semi submerged and harking to the archaeological finds it houses, the museum reveals the recognizable long warehouse typology only from the higher south elevation. Yet as the site slopes away on the north side the true nature of the hexagonal shape is exposed.

Ai Weiweis Beitrag zu den siebzehn Pavillons des Jinhua Architectural Park ist das Museum für antikes chinesisches Porzellan. Der Entwurf spielt mit Tradition und Abstraktion und entstammt dem regionalen Haustyp, bestehend aus Wänden und einem Satteldach. Das Gebäude besitzt aufgrund seines sechseckigen Querschnitts einen stark wieder erkennbaren Charakter und fügt sich subtil in die Landschaft ein. Halb eingegraben und in Anlehnung an die archäologischen Funde, die es beherbergt, offenbart sich die lange Lagerhaustypologie des Museums nur von der Süderhebung. Auf der abfallenden Nordseite kommt die wahre Natur der sechseckigen Form zu Tage.

De los diecisiete pabellones del Jinhua Architectural
Park, Ai Weiwei se ha ocupado del diseño del museo de
cerámicas antiguas chinas. Jugando entre la tradición
y la abstracción su diseño recoge la típica estructura
de la casa vernacular con paredes y tejado en declive.
Debido a su forma hexagonal con sección en cruz, el
edificio es claramente reconocible. El museo, sutilmente,
se integra en el paisaje. La construcción semienterrada,
evocando los hallazgos arqueológicos que alberga,
revela la típica estructura alargada de almacén solo
desde la zona meridional más elevada y – puesto que el
lugar presenta una inclinación – desde el lado norte se
ve muy claramente la verdadera naturaleza del diseño
hexagonal.

Parmi le dix-sept pavillons qui composent le Jinhua
Architectural Park, Weiwei s'est occupé du projet du
musée des anciennes céramiques chinoises. En jouant
avec tradition et abstraction, son design reproduit la
structure typique des maisons vernaculaires avec murs
et toit en pente. Grâce à la section transversale hexagonale le bâtiment est très reconnaissable. Le musée
se mêle avec le paysage environnant. La construction
demi-enterrée, qui évoque les pièces archéologiques
qu'elle héberge, dévoile la typique forme allongée d'un
entrepôt juste de la zone sud la plus élevée et comme le
terrain est en pente, du coté nord on voit clairement la
vraie nature de la forme hexagonale.

Dei diciasette padiglioni del Jinhua Architectural Park, Ai Weiwei ha curato la progettazione del museo delle ceramiche antiche cinesi. Giocando con tradizione e astrazione, il progetto riprende la tipica struttura della casa vernacolare con muri e tetto spiovente. L'edificio risulta molto riconoscibile a causa della sezione trasversale esagonale e si inserisca perfettamente nel paesaggio circostante. La costruzione semi-interrata, rieccheggiante i ritrovamenti archeologici che ospita, svela la caratteristica tipologia allungata di magazzino soltanto dalla zona meridionale più elevata. Poiché il terreno è in pendenza, dal lato nord è chiaramente visibile la vera natura della forma esagonale.

"新石器时代陶器博物馆" 在金华建筑艺术公园内的17个展览馆，艾未未设计了"中国古代陶器博物馆"。设计介于传统与抽象之间，从具有本国风格的墙壁到建有人形墙的屋顶演化而来。由于其外形具有高度代表性，博物馆 与周围的风景微妙的融合到一起。平面设计为六边形。在该建筑内，可以隐隐沉浸在考古发现中，仿佛在倾听它们，也只有在地势较高的南面才能看出博物馆建筑那长长的、形似仓库般的外形。然而，由于北面的斜坡，六边形的外形才得到了真实的展现。

NINE BOXES
ART GALLERIES & OFFICES
BEIJING, CHINA
Design date: 03–05.2004
Construction date: 08–09.2004
Total floor area: 2.751 m²

The complex comprises nine metal boxes, which seem more akin to an installation rather than to architecture. The challenge of transforming existing houses into art galleries and office spaces within a limited budget and timeframe was solved with a light steel structure wrapped with a galvanized steel skin. The existing buildings with their pitched roofs were enclosed by simple metal boxes and thus stripped of their original form.

Der Komplex umfasst neun Metallboxen, die eher eine Installation als Architektur zu sein scheinen. Die Herausforderung, vorhandene Häuser in Kunstgalerien und Büroräume mit einem beschränkten Budget und Zeitrahmen umzugestalten, wurde mithilfe einer leichten, galvanisierten Stahlstruktur gelöst. Die vorhandenen Strukturen mit ihren aufgestellten Dächern wurden von einfachen Metallboxen eingeschlossen und so ihrer ursprünglichen Form beraubt.

El complejo comprende nueve cajas metálicas, más cercanas al concepto de instalación que al de arquitectura. El reto de querer transformar las casas existentes en galerías de arte y espacios para oficinas, teniendo a disposición un presupuesto reducido y un tiempo limitado, fue acogido empleando una ligera estructura de acero revestida de acero galvanizado. Las estructuras existentes con sus tejados inclinados fueron encerradas en sencillas cajas de metal y por tanto despojadas de su forma original.

L'ensemble comprend neuf boîtes métalliques qui évoquent le concept d'installation beaucoup plus que celui d'architecture. Le défi de transformer les maisons existantes en galeries et espaces bureaux avec un budget réduit et un temps limité à disposition a été relevé en utilisant une structure légère en acier, revêtue d'acier galvanisé. Les structures existantes aux toits inclinés ont été renfermées en simples boîtes métalliques et ont perdu donc leur forme originelle.

Il complesso comprende nove cubi metallici, più vicini al concetto d'installazione che a quello d' architettura. La sfida nel voler trasformare le case esistenti in gallerie e spazi per uffici avendo a disposizione un budget ridotto e un tempo limitato è stata raccolta utilizzando una leggera struttura metallica rivestita di acciaio galvanizzato. Le strutture esistenti con i loro tetti inclinati sono state racchiuse in semplici scatole di metallo e di conseguenza strappate alla loro forma originale.

"九个盒子" 复合建筑由9个金属盒子组成，看上去更像是装置，而非建筑。以有限的资金在有限的时间内将现有的房屋改造成艺术画廊和办公区是一项挑战，但包裹着镀锌铁皮的轻型钢结构解决了这一问题。原本涂有沥青的屋顶包上了设计简单的金属盒子，从而改变了原有面貌。传统房屋与如此简单的立体盒子并列使得毫无所知的游客感到震撼。

GO WHERE
RESTAURANT | BEIJING, CHINA
Design date: 2004
Construction date: 10.2004
Total floor area: 230 m²

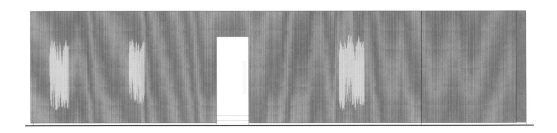

It is a renovation of an old building with a significant newly constructed part. The new outer wall made up of laminated cement fiberboards inlaid with glass panels and steel plates acts as both the structure and finish. The muted transparency of stacked glass panels within the fiberboard wall contributes to the restaurant's dimmed atmosphere. The entire project was completed in only fourty days.

Ein altes Gebäude wurde renoviert und um einen Neubau erweitert. Die neue Außenwand, die aus laminierten Zementholzfaserplatten besteht, in die Glastafeln und Stahlelemente eingelassen sind, ist sowohl Struktur als auch Oberfläche. Die gedämpfte Transparenz der Glaspanele im Inneren der Holzfaserplattenwand trägt zur verdunkelten Atmosphäre im Restaurant bei. Das komplette Projekt wurde in nur vierzig Tagen vollendet.

Se trata de la renovación de un viejo edificio con una amplia zona construida ex-novo. La nueva pared exterior, formada por placas de fibrocemento laminado combinadas con paneles de cristal y planchas de acero, hace las veces tanto de estructura como de acabado. La transparencia mutante obtenida con los paneles de cristal en el interior de la pared crea un ambiente de luz difuminada por todo el restaurante. El proyecto ha sido terminado por completo en solo cuarenta días.

Il s'agit de la restructuration d'un vieux bâtiment à travers la construction d'une ample zone nouvelle. Le nouveau mur extérieur, composé par des plaques en béton laminées avec panneaux en verre et plaques en acier, a la fonction de structure aussi bien que de finition. La transparence adoucie, obtenue grâce aux panneaux en verre à l'intérieur de la paroi, crée une atmosphère de lumière diffuse dans tout le restaurant. Le projet a été complété entièrement en quarante jours seulement.

Si tratta di una ristrutturazione di un vecchio edificio con un'ampia zona costruita ex novo. Il nuovo muro esterno, composto da lastre in fibrocemento laminate abbinate a pannelli di vetro e placche di acciaio, rappresenta sia la struttura, sia la rifinitura. La trasparenza attenuata dei pannelli di vetro all'interno della parete crea un'atmosfera di luce soffusa all'interno del ristorante. L'intero progetto è stato completato in soli quaranta giorni.

"去哪餐厅" 该餐厅是一座由老建筑翻新并加盖了一个重要的部分而构成的。新建筑外墙由薄片状的水泥纤维板制成，嵌入了钢板和玻璃。玻璃板与钢板即可以作为结构材料，又可以作为内部/外部的磨光漆。纤维墙内部堆积的玻璃板使得透明度更加柔和，为餐厅营造了朦胧的氛围。整个项目仅用四十天就完成。

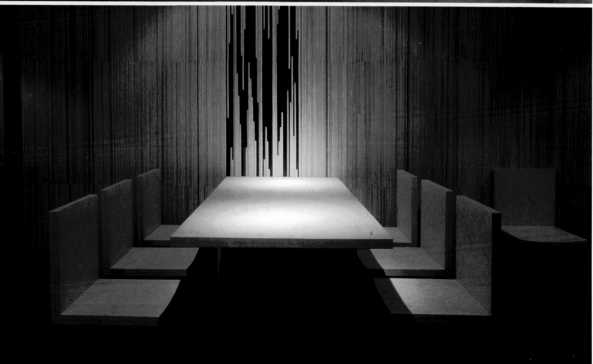

CUO HOUSE
RESIDENTIAL BUILDING
BEIJING, CHINA
Unrealized
Design date: 07 – 11.2004
Area: 1.120 m²

Cuo is a way of arranging displacement through shifting and twisting while multiplying an identical component, in order to make them into a harmonic entity. The house is made out of eight T-shapes walls. On the ground floor, each of the four T-shapes has a 90° displacement to the centre. On the second level, the additional four T-shapes flip over to form the upper level structure. The enclosed space formed in the center becomes the private courtyard. From its diagrammatic appearance, the Cuo House has the characteristics of the traditional Chinese courtyard house. In addition, the hierarchy of the house follows a logic which uses the displacement of a simple shape to separate the public and private and to define interior and exterior. It also gives the momentum to the interior structure underneath its rigid body. While the T-structures describe large zones, a second structure of serving walls, which may contain installation, forms smaller, more intimate spaces. A part of this second structure is made of translucent glass walls. Rooms of different spatial qualities: narrow, long, wide and small - follow each other, so that the visitor gradually inhabits the space. Just as the whole concept, its logic and structure has to do with a diagonal organization.

Cuo bedeutet, Versetzung durch Verschiebung und Drehung zu arrangieren, indem ein identischer Bestandteil multipliziert wird, um eine harmonische Einheit daraus zu machen. Das Haus besteht aus acht T-förmigen Wänden, die auf zwei Geschossen gleichmäßig verteilt sind. Im Erdgeschoss sind die vier Wände um 90° zum Zentrum versetz. Im Obergeschoss bilden vier zusätzliche gedrehte Wände die obere Geschossstruktur. Der umschlossene zentrale Raum wird zum privaten Innenhof. In seiner schematischen Erscheinung ähnelt das Cuo Haus dem traditionellen chinesischen Hofhaus. Zusätzlich folgt die Gebäudehierarchie einer Logik, die das Versetzen einer einfachen Form nutzt, um öffentliche und private Bereiche zu trennen und Innen und Außen zu definieren. Ausserdem gibt dies auch den Innenräumen einen gewissen Schwung unter dem starren Körper. Während die T-Strukturen breite Zonen beschreiben, formt eine zweite Schicht aus Installationswänden kleinere, vertraute Räume. Ein Teil dieser zweiten Struktur besteht aus lichtdurchlässigen Glaswänden. Räume unterschiedlicher Qualitäten, schmal, lang, breit, klein folgen aufeinander, sodass der Besucher allmählich den Raum bewohnt. Das ganze Konzept, seine Logik und die Struktur basieren auf einer diagonalen Organisation.

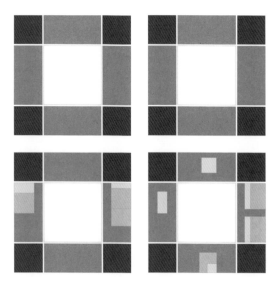

Cuo es una forma de organizar el desplazamiento en el espacio moviendo y girando un mismo componente multiplicado varias veces, hasta obtener una entidad armoniosa. La casa está formada por ocho paredes con forma de T. En la planta baja, cada una de las cuatro formas de T tiene un desplazamiento de 90° respecto al centro, mientras que en el segundo piso las restantes cuatro formas de T giran hasta formar la estructura del piso superior. El espacio que queda encerrado en el centro es lo que forma el patio privado. El aspecto esquemático de la Cuo House recoge las características de la típica casa china con patio. Además, según la lógica jerarquica de la casa, el desplazamiento de una simple forma sirve para separar la zona pública de la privada. Esto atribuye impulso a la estructura interior debajo del cuerpo rígido. Mientras las estructuras con forma de T describen amplias zonas, una segunda estructura de paredes divisorias, que pueden contener eventuales instalaciones, forman espacios más pequeños y más íntimos. Una parte de estas estructuras está realizada en cristal traslúcido. Las habitaciones, con diferentes características espaciales – estrechas, largas, amplias, pequeñas – se siguen unas a otras permitiendo al visitante adueñarse del espacio de forma gradual. Exactamente como todo el proyecto por completo, su lógica y su estructura tienen que ver con la organización diagonal del espacio.

Cuo est une façon d'organiser la distribution dans l'espace en déplaçant et en tournant une composante identique répétée plusieurs fois jusqu'à obtenir une entité harmonieuse. La maison se compose par huit murs en forme de T. Au rez-de-chaussée, chacune des quatre formes à T est écartée de 90° par rapport au centre, tandis que, au deuxième étage, les quatre formes à T restantes tournent jusqu'à dessiner la structure de l'étage supérieur. L'espace qui se forme au milieu crée une cour privée. L'aspect schématique de la Cuo House imite les caractéristiques de la typique maison chinoise avec cour. En plus, selon la logique de hiérarchie de la maison, la répétition d'une seule forme sert à séparer la zone publique de celle privée et à définir des zones internes et externes en donnant plus d'élan à la structure interne au dessous de son corps rigide. Si les structures à T dessinent des zones plus amples, une deuxième structure de cloisons, qui peuvent contenir éventuellement des installations, forme des espaces plus intimes et plus petits. Une partie de ces structures est réalisée en verre transparent. Les chambres, qui ont les caractéristique spatiales les plus diverses – étroites, longues, amples, petites – se succèdent l'une après l'autre en permettant au visiteur de s'approprier graduellement de l'espace. Exactement comme pour le reste du projet, sa logique et sa structure se focalisent sur l'organisation de l'espace en diagonale.

Cuo è un modo di organizzare la dislocazione nello spazio spostando e ruotando un'identica componente più volte replicata, fino ad ottenere un'entità armonica. La casa è composta da otto muri a forma di T. Al piano terra, ciascuna delle quattro forme a T ha uno scostamento di 90° rispetto al centro, mentre, al secondo piano, le rimanenti quattro forme a T ruotano così da formare la struttura del piano superiore. Lo spazio che si racchiude al centro crea il cortile privato. L'aspetto schematico della Cuo House riprende le caratteristiche della tipica casa cinese con cortile. In aggiunta, secondo la logica di gerarchia della casa, la dislocazione di una semplice forma serve a separare la zona pubblica da quella privata e a definire zone interne ed esterne, attribuendo inoltre slancio alla struttura interna sotto il suo corpo rigido. Mentre le strutture a T creano delle zone più ampie, una seconda struttura di pareti divisorie, che possono contenere eventuali installazioni, forma spazi più piccoli e più intimi. Una parte di queste strutture è realizzata in vetro traslucido. Le stanze, dalle diverse caratteristiche spaziali - strette, lunghe, ampie, piccole - si susseguono una dopo l'altra, permettendo al visitatore di appropriarsi gradatamente dello spazio. Proprio come il progetto completo, la sua logica e la sua struttura si focalizzano sull'organizzazione diagonale dello spazio.

"错屋" "错"是在反复使用同一种结构时，通过变换与扭转来安排位移，达到的整体和谐效果的方法。该房屋由八面T型墙构成。一楼的四面墙各向中心错位90度。二楼的另外四面T型墙翻转后构成上层结构。而中间封闭的区域则成为了私人庭院。"错屋"的大致外形具有中国传统庭院的特色。另外，房屋的层级设计也具有逻辑性，通过简单形状的错位将公共区域与私人空间隔开，并区分内部与外部。这就在刻板的主体结构下赋予其内部以动态力量。T型墙结构占去了大部分区域，而在第二种墙壁结构装配之后，获得了更加狭小而私密的空间。该结构的部分是玻璃墙。各种具有不同空间特性的房间，或窄或长，或宽或小，一间紧靠另一间，这样客人可以逐渐体验整个空间。与该建筑的整体概念一样，对角形组合设计受到了逻辑与结构的影响。

COURTYARD 105
OFFICE AND HOUSING
CAOCHANGDI, BEIJING, CHINA
Design date: 10.2004
Construction date: 10.2004 – 04.2005
Total site area: 3.044 m²

Starting from pre-existing one-story office spaces that were built in the village's vernacular style, the architect preserved the majority of the original volumes and converted them into living units, offices and a dance studio. Two one-story structures attached to the existing building form a private exterior space within the semiprivate court. Two other simple, rectangular, one-room buildings complete the extension. A double-height briefing room is located in the courtyard's center to block site lines into the court. New and existing buildings are knitted together by the use of the same blue-gray brick. The proportions of the new windows and openings, the material, and spatial structure orchestrate the assimilation of the different elements of the complex.

Ausgehend von den vorhandenen einstöckigen, im einheimischen Dorfstil gebauten Büroräumen, bewahrte der Architekt die Mehrheit der originalen Baukörper und wandelte sie in Wohneinheiten, Büros und ein Tanzstudio um. Zwei einstöckige, dem vorhandenen Gebäude angefügte Strukturen, bilden einen privaten Außenraum innerhalb des halbprivaten Innenhofs. Zwei weitere, einfache, rechteckige Ein-Raum-Bauten schließen die Erweiterung ab. Ein Besprechungszimmer mit doppelter Raumhöhe liegt mitten im Hof und begrenzt dessen Seitenlinien. Neue und alte Gebäude werden durch den Gebrauch desselben blau-grauen Ziegels zusammengehalten. Die Proportionen der neuen Fenster und Öffnungen, das Material und die Raumstruktur fügen die verschiedenen Komplexelemente harmonisch zusammen.

A partir de espacios preexistentes de oficina de un solo piso construidos en el típico estilo vernacular del pueblo, el arquitecto ha conservado la mayor parte de los volúmenes originales convirtiéndolos en unidades habitables, oficinas y una escuela de danza. Dos estructuras mono-piso, unidas al edificio existente, forman un espacio externo privado, en el interior del patio semiprivado. Otras dos construcciones sencillas, rectangulares de un espacio único completan el complejo. En el centro del patio se encuentra una sala de reuniones de doble altura, como límite de las líneas laterales del patio. Edificios viejos y nuevos se unen utilizando para ello los mismos ladrillos gris-azulados. Las proporciones de las nuevas ventanas y de las aberturas, el material y la estructura espacial, orquestan la asimilación de los diferentes elementos del complejo.

En partant de la structure préexistante avec des espaces bureaux sur un étage dans le style vernaculaire typique du village, l'architecte a gardé la majorité des volumes originaux et les a convertis en unités d'habitation, bureaux et une école de danse. Deux structures à un seul étage, ajoutées au bâtiment existant, forment un espace interne privé à l'intérieur de la cour semi-privée. Deux autres constructions simples, rectangulaires, avec une seule chambre, complètent l'extension. Au milieu de la cour il y a une salle de réunion à double hauteur qui limite les lignes latérales de la cour. De nouveaux bâtiments se mêlent aux vieux grâce à l'emploi des mêmes briques gris-bleu. Les proportions des nouvelles fenêtres et des ouvertures, le matériau et à la structure de l'espace se mélangent afin d'assimiler les différents éléments de l'ensemble de façon harmonieuse.

Da preesistenti spazi adibiti ad ufficio ad un piano, costruiti nel tipico stile vernacolare del villaggio, l'architetto ha conservato la maggior parte dei volumi originali convertendoli in unità abitative, uffici e in una scuola di danza. Due strutture a un solo piano, annesse all'edificio esistente, formano uno spazio esterno privato all'interno del cortile semi-privato. Altre due costruzioni semplici, rettangolari, con un'unico spazio, completano l'estensione. Al centro del cortile si trova una sala riunioni a doppia altezza, posta come limite delle linee laterali del cortile. Edifici vecchi e nuovi vengono uniti grazie all'utilizzo dello stesso mattone grigio-blu. Le proporzioni delle nuove finestre e delle aperture si combinano ai materiali e alla struttura dello spazio per assimilare in modo armonioso i diversi elementi del complesso.

"105号院子" 建筑师从村子里现有的本地风格单层办公区着手，保留了大部分原有建筑，将它们改造成起居单元，办公室和舞蹈房。在原有建筑的基础上增建了两座单层建筑，在半私人的院子里构成私人的外部空间。扩建内容还包括其它两座简单的矩形单间房。双倍高度的会客室 被安排在庭院中间，挡住了投向院内的视线。扩建及原有建筑通过使用相同的蓝灰砖块而融合在一起。新窗户的比例及开口，用料及空间结构得到精心安排，从而使得该复合建筑的不同成份得以同化。

COURTYARD 104
GALLERY
CAOCHANGDI, BEIJING, CHINA
Design date: 09.2005
Construction date: 11.2005
Total built area: 1.565 m²

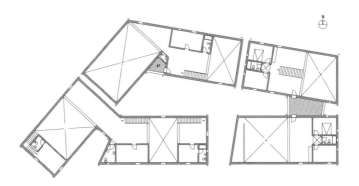

Designed to be a gallery, Courtyard 104 consists of two-story buildings that are broken up primarily on the ground level only. The woven interior circulation creates private zones and mezzanines overlooking the double-height ateliers and attached living units. Skylight illuminates the work spaces. An enclosure wall of vernacular brick lattice work dampens street noise and a small maintenance alley runs between it and the neighboring buildings. 70% of the bricks used for the façade are blue-gray and 30% are red. Entering the courtyard, the visitor is immediately confronted with a two-story volume extending itself, creating a canopy that funnels the visitor into the courtyard's interior. Unadorned walls, ceilings, and floors affirm the materiality of their construction: humble concrete and bricks.

Die Galerie besteht aus zweistöckigen Gebäuden, die in erster Linie nur im Erdgeschoss aufgebrochen sind. Der verwobene innere Umlauf schafft private Bereiche und Zwischengeschosse, von denen aus man die doppelte Raumhöhe der Ateliers und die angefügten Wohneinheiten überblickt. Dachfenster belichten die Arbeitsbereiche. Eine Mauer aus einheimischer Ziegelgitterarbeit dämpft die Straßengeräusche und eine kleine Wartungsallee läuft zwischen dieser und den benachbarten Gebäuden. 70% der Fassadenziegel sind blau-grau und 30% rot ausgeführt. Beim Betreten des Innenhofs steht der Besucher einem zweistöckigen Volumen unmittelbar gegenüber, das sich trichterförmig erweitert und so ein Vordach erzeugt, das einen ins Hofinnere leitet. Schmucklose Wände, Decken, und Fußböden unterstreichen die Materialität ihrer Konstruktion: Einfacher Beton und Ziegel.

Ideada en principio como galería, Courtyard 104 está formada por edificios de dos pisos en los que esencialmente sólo la planta baja ha sido dividida. La circulación interna tramada crea zonas privadas y entresuelos que se asoman a talleres de doble altura y a las unidades habitables adyacentes. Un tragaluz ilumina los espacios de trabajo. Una tapia de ladrillo vernacular atenúa el ruido de la calle y un pequeño caminito de servicio discurre entre el muro y las construcciones cercanas. El 70% de los ladrillos empleados para la fachada son gris-azulados y el 30% rojos. Entrando en el patio, el visitante se encuentra de frente a un volumen de dos plantas que se extiende creando un pasillo cuberto que le conduce al patio interior. Los techos, los suelos, las paredes sin adornos vuelven a confirmar los materiales de la construcción: humilde hormigón y ladrillos.

Conçue pour être une galerie, Courtyard 104 se compose par des bâtiments à deux étages dont seulement le rez-de-chaussée a été ouvert. La circulation interne crée des zones privées et des mezzanines qui donnent sur les ateliers à double hauteur et sur les unités d'habitation adjacentes. Une lucarne éclaire les espaces de travail. Un mur d'enceinte à claie de briques vernaculaires assourdit le bruit de la rue et une petite allée de service court entre le mur et les bâtiments à coté. 70% des briques employés pour la façade sont gris-bleu et 30% sont rouges. En entrant dans la cour, le visiteur se trouve en face d'une volumétrie à deux étages qui s'étend en créant un entonnoir dont le bout mène dans la cour interne. Les plafonds, les sols, les murs nus confirment la matérialité du bâtiment : humble béton et briques.

Ideata come galleria, Courtyard 104 è costituita da edifici a due piani di cui essenzialmente solo il piano terra è stato aperto. La circolazione interna ad intreccio crea zone private e dei mezzanini che si affacciano sui laboratori dalla doppia altezza e sulle unità abitative adiacenti. Un lucernario illumina gli spazi di lavoro. Un muro di cinta a graticcio di mattone vernacolare attutisce il rumore della strada e un piccolo vialetto di servizio corre tra il muro e le vicine costruzioni. Il 70% dei mattoni utilizzati per la facciata sono grigio-blu e il 30% rossi. Entrando nel cortile, il visitatore si trova di fronte ad una volumetria a due piani che si estende creando un tunnel ad imbuto, la cui estremità conduce nel cortile interno. I soffitti, i pavimenti, i muri disadorni riconfermano la materialità della costruzione: umile calcestruzzo e mattoni.

"104号院子" 104号院子设计为画廊，由多幢两层建筑组成，它们只在地面相互独立。内部走廊交叉在一起，创造了私人的区域和包厢，俯瞰双倍高的画室和附属起居单元。天窗透进的阳光为工作区提供照明。本土风格的砖块格子围墙减弱了街道噪音，一道小型生活走廊将它与周围的建筑连接起来。正面墙的70%用料为蓝灰色砖，其余30%为红砖。进入庭院，游客会立即看到一座双层的建筑延伸开去，形成一座遮篷，将游客引入庭院内部。未经装饰的墙壁，天花板及地板证明建筑材料为普通的混凝土，砖块及涂料。

COLA HOUSE
HANGZHOU, ZHEJIANG, CHINA
Cooperation with Wang Shu
Design date: 12.2005
Construction date: 12.2005

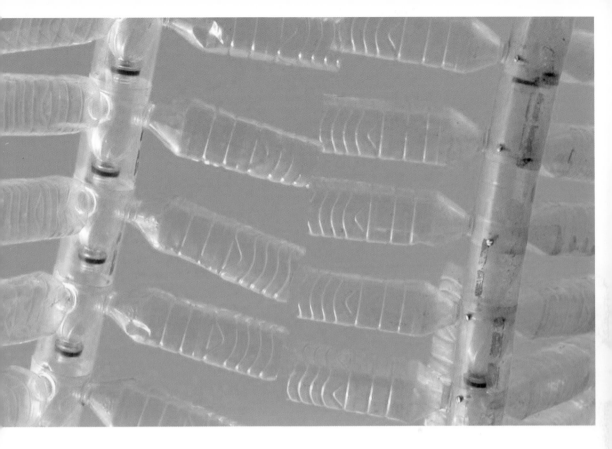

This project was assisted by the China Academy of Art's architecture students from the class of 2005 and was called "1:1 architecture". Using plastic bottles and metal fasteners, the Cola House is a testament to the notion of reuse where one mans trash is another mans treasure.

Architektur-Studenten des Jahrgangs 2005 der China Academy of Art halfen mit bei dem Projekt mit dem Namen „1:1 Architektur", bei dem Plastikflaschen und Metallverschlüsse engesetzt wurden. Das Cola-Haus ist ein Testament zum Begriff des Widergebrauchs. Eines Menschen Abfall, ist des anderen Menschen Schatz.

Este proyecto ha sido realizado en colaboración con los estudiantes de arquitectura de la China Academy of Art, clase del 2005, y titulado "Arquitectura 1:1". Empleando botellas de plástico y enganches de metal, la Cola House constituye una reafirmación del concepto de reutilización: lo que una persona descarta se convierte en tesoro para otra.

Ce projet a été réalisé en collaboration avec les étudiants d'architecture de la China Academy of Art de l'année universitaire 2005, titré « Architecture 1:1 ». Avec ses bouteilles en plastique et ses agrafes en métal, la Cola House constitue une réaffirmation du concept de réemploi, selon lequel ce qui est déchet pour un homme devient un trésor pour un autre.

Questo progetto è stato realizzato in collaborazione con gli studenti di architettura della China Academy of Art dell'anno accademico 2005 ed intitolato "Architettura 1:1". Utilizzando bottiglie di plastica e fermagli in metallo, la Cola House costituisce una riaffermazione del concetto di riutilizzo, secondo cui, ciò che è scarto per qualcuno, rappresenta un tesoro per un altro.

"可乐房" 该项目由中国艺术学院建筑系2005届学生协助完成，称为1:1建筑。"可乐房" 用料为塑料瓶及金属扣件，是对再利用概念的一次检验，在那里废品变为宝贝。

TREE HOUSE
GUESTHOUSE FOR A GOLF CLUB
LIJIANG, YUNNAN, CHINA
Cooperation with HHF architects
Design date: 03 – 11.2005
Construction date: 04.2006 – 01.2007
Total floor area: 400 m²

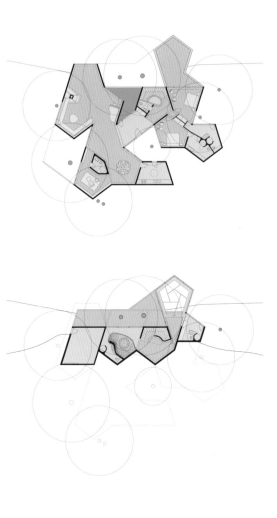

The layout of the Tree House is based on a pentagonal pattern. An interesting concept as there is no possibility of creating an infinite addition of pentagons without having leftovers which are essential for the layout, as they create special light situations, link the interior to the surrounding nature and integrate the existing trees into the house. Like leaves forming a space underneath a tree, light and shadow become fundamental elements for different space qualities. The house is organized on two levels and partially cantilevers over the water of the lake. The complexity of the geometry stands in contrast to the simplicity of the materials and details. A very soft looking concrete cast with bamboo boarding is used inside and outside. For assimilating the house into nature, the roof is covered with grass.

Die Baumhausstruktur beruht auf einem fünfeckigen Muster. Ein interessantes Konzept, weil es nicht möglich ist, eine unendliche Ansammlung von Fünfecken zu schaffen, ohne Überreste zu haben. Diese wiederum sind für den Grundriss notwendig, da sie eine spezielle Leichtigkeit erzeugen, das Innere mit der Umgebung verbinden und die vorhandenen Bäume ins Haus integrieren. Wie Blätter einen Raum unterm Baum formen, ermöglichen Licht und Schatten verschiedene Raumqualitäten. Das zweistöckige Haus ragt teilweise über das Wasser aus. Der komplexen Geometrie stehen einfache Materialien und Details gegenüber. Eine sehr weich wirkende Betonverschalung aus Bambusplatten kam sowohl innen als auch außen zum Einsatz. Um das Haus an die umgebende Natur anzupassen, wurde das Dach begrünt.

El proyecto de la Tree House se basa en un patrón pentagonal. Concepto muy interesante, puesto que no hay posibilidad de crear una agregación infinita de pentágonos sin dejar espacios residuales que resultan esenciales para el proyecto, entanto que éstos crean juegos de luces especiales, vinculan uniones entre el ambiente interno con el de los alrededores, así como con las plantas que ya existían en el interior de la casa. Como hojas que crean un espacio bajo el árbol, luces y sombras se convierten en elementos fundamentales para delinear diferentes cualidades de espacio. La casa está organizada en dos niveles y en parte vuela sobre la superficie del lago. La complejidad de su geometría contrasta con la sencillez de los materiales y de los detalles. En el interior y en el exterior se utllizò hormigón de apariencia muy suave, encofrado con bambú. Para integrar mejor la casa con la naturaleza que la rodea, el tejado se ha recubierto con hierba.

Le projet de la Tree House se base sur un schéma pentagonal. Il s'agit ici d'une conception intéressante, parce que on ne peut pas créer une agrégation infinie de pentagones sans laisser des espaces vides qui sont essentiels pour le projet, vu qu'ils créent des jeux de lumières spéciales et des liens entre l'environnement interne et celui entourant, en intégrant les plantes pré-existantes à la maison. Ainsi que les feuilles qui créent un espace sous l'arbre, lumière et ombre deviennent deux éléments fondamentaux pour délinéer des qualités d'espaces différentes. La maison est organisée sur deux niveaux et se penche sur la surface du lac. La complexité de sa géométrie est en contraste avec la simplicité des matériaux et des détails. L'intérieur et l'extérieur sont en béton visuellement très léger moulé avec des cloisons en planches de bambou. Pour mieux uniformiser la maison avec la nature, le toit a été recouvert d'herbe.

Il progetto della Tree House si basa su uno schema pentagonale. Un concetto molto interessante, poiché non vi è possibile creare un'aggregazione infinita di pentagoni senza lasciare dei vuoti che risultano essenziali per il progetto, in quanto creano speciali giochi di luce e collegamenti tra l'ambiente interno e quello circostante, integrando le piante esistenti nella la casa. Così come le foglie creano uno spazio sotto l'albero, luce ed ombra divengono elementi fondamentali per delineare differenti qualità di spazio. La casa è organizzata su due livelli e in parte si protende sulla superficie del lago. La complessità della sua geometria contrasta con la semplicità dei materiali e dei dettagli. L'interno e l'esterno sono di un calcestruzzo apparentemente molto leggero modellato a forma di assito in bambù. Per meglio uniformare la casa con la natura, il tetto è stato ricoperto d'erba.

"树屋" 树屋的布局基于五边形。该建筑布局的核心是一个有趣的概念，即：绝无可能创造出一个无限的五边形集合体而不产生剩余空间。他们创造出独特的照明布局，将建筑内部与周围自然环境连接起来，并将原有的树木与房屋整合到一起。正如树叶在其下方形成的空间，光线和阴影成为不同空间特质的基础原素。房屋设计成两层，且部分悬于湖面上方。复杂的几何构造与用料及细节方面的简约形成对比。建筑内外都使用竹板制成，看上去十分柔和。屋顶用草覆盖使得房屋与自然融为了一体。

SIX ROOMS
RESIDENTIAL BUILDING
NANJING, JIANGSU, CHINA
Under construction
Design date: 2004
Total floor area: 600 m²

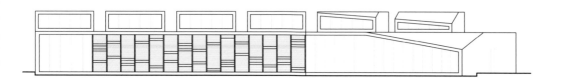

This building is composed of six working rooms and a corridor that develops into a living room. A loop, glazed on two sides, forms the corridor and living room. The use of materials is reduced to concrete, wood fins, plasterboard and glass. The glazing of the rooms is oriented to the north. Wood fins mark the threshold from corridor to living room.

Das Gebäude besteht aus sechs Arbeitsräumen und einem Wohnzimmer, das sich aus einem Gang entwickelt. Eine schleifenartige, natürlich belichtete Struktur bildet den Gang und das Wohnzimmer. Die Materialien beschränken sich auf Beton, Holzplanken, Gipsplatten und Glas. Die Räume sind auf der Nordseite verglast. Holzplanken kennzeichnen die Schwelle vom Gang ins Wohnzimmer.

Este edificio está formado por seis salas de trabajo y un corredor que se extiende en una sala de estar. Un cordón anular, iluminado desde ambos lados, forma el pasillo y la sala de estar. El empleo de materiales se limita a hormigón, aletas de madera, paneles de cartón-yeso y cristal. Las superficies acristaladas de las habitaciones están orientadas hacia el norte. Los aletas de madera delinean el umbral de entrada desde el pasillo hasta la sala de estar.

Ce bâtiment se compose de six zones de travail et un séjour qui se développe comme agrandissement d'un couloir. L'emploi de matériaux se limite au béton, aux plaques en bois, au placoplâtre et au verre. Les baies vitrées du salon sont orientées à nord. Une structure circulaire, éclairée sur les deux cotés, forme un couloir et le séjour, dont le seuil est délimité par des plaques en bois.

Questo edificio è costituito da sei ambienti lavorativi ed un soggiorno che si sviluppa come ampliamento di un corridoio. L'utilizzo dei materiali si limita a calcestruzzo, lamine di legno, cartongesso e vetro. Le vetrate delle stanze sono orientate a nord. Una struttura circolare, illuminata da entrambi i lati, forma il corridoio ed il soggiorno, la cui soglia viene marcata da lamine di legno.

"六间" 该建筑由六间工作室和一间由走廊改建而来的客厅组成。用材仅为水泥，木鳍板，石灰板和玻璃。房间的北面装上了玻璃。环形线路的两边装上了玻璃，作为走廊与客厅。木鳍板则作为走廊与客厅的分界线。

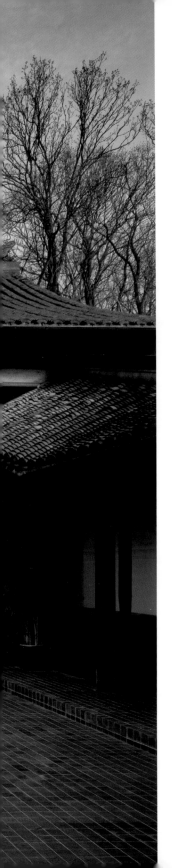

JIANGNANHUI
BUSINESS CLUB
HANGZHOU, ZHEJIANG, CHINA
Design date: 08.2006 – 02.2007
Construction date: 04 – 11.2007
Total site area: 7.876 m²
Total built area: 2.500 m²

This project converted seven traditionally styled villas into a luxury club. The idea was to replace the façades in order to create consistency. The redesign of the façades provided the villas with a contemporary interior quality without completely abandoning the traditional aesthetics. The new façades have a system of layers in order to control temperature, privacy and light. The outermost layer required the production of more than seven hundred intricately joined wood screens. Transcendent of the divisions of function, the wood screens are continuous. The seven villas were divided into four private suites, a restaurant, a spa, a tea house, a night bar, meeting halls and administrative spaces.

Dieses Projekt wandelte sieben, im traditionellen Stil entworfene Villen, in einen Luxusklub um. Die Idee war, die Fassaden zu ersetzen, um Konsistenz zu schaffen. Die Umgestaltung der Fassaden versorgte die Villen mit einer zeitgenössischen Innenqualität, ohne dabei die traditionellen Eigenschaften völlig aufzugeben. Die neuen Fassaden bestehen aus verschiedenen Schichten, um Temperatur, private Atmosphäre und Licht zu beeinflussen. Für die äußerste Schicht wurden mehr als siebenhundert, kompliziert verbundene Holzwände produziert. Unabhängig von den unterschiedlichen Funktionen, sind die Holzwände durchgängig. Die sieben Villen wurden in vier private Suiten, ein Restaurant, ein Spa, ein Teehaus, eine Bar und Besprechungs- und Verwaltungsräume aufgeteilt.

El proyecto ha transformado siete casas de campo de estilo tradicional en un club de lujo. La idea fue la de sustituir las fachadas para así crear coherencia. El nuevo proyecto dotó a las casas de campo de cualidades contemporáneas internas sin abandonar completamente la estética tradicional. Las nuevas fachadas consisten en un sistema de capas para el control de la temperatura, de la intimidad y de la luz. Para componer la capa más externa ha sido necesario producir más de setecientas pantallas de madera unidas de forma compleja. Independientemente de la división de las funciones, las pantallas de madera siguen sin interrupción. Las siete casas de campo fueron divididas en cuatro suites privadas, un restaurante, un spa, una casa de té, un night bar, lugares de encuentro y espacios administrativos.

Le projet a transformé sept maisons en style traditionnel en un club de luxe. L'idée consista à remplacer les façades afin de créer de la cohérence. Le nouveau projet donna aux villas des intérieurs de qualité contemporaine sans abandonner complètement l'esthétique traditionnelle. Les nouvelles façades se composent d'un système de couches afin de contrôler la température, l'intimité et la lumière. Pour composer la couche la plus externe, il a fallu produire plus de sept cent paravents en bois raccordés de façon complexe. Indépendamment de la répartition des fonctions, les paravents en bois se succèdent sans interruptions. Les sept maisons furent subdivisées en quatre suites privées, un restaurant, une Spa, une maison de thé et un night club, lieux de rencontre et espaces administratifs.

Il progetto ha trasformato sette ville in stile tradizionale in un club di lusso. L'idea fu quella di sostituire le facciate così da creare coerenza. Il nuovo progetto donò alle ville interni di qualità contemporanea senza abbandonare completamente l'estetica tradizionale. Le nuove facciate consistono in un sistema di strati, finalizzato al controllo della temperatura, della privacy e della luce. Per comporre lo strato più esterno è stato necessario produrre più di sette cento paraventi in legno uniti in modo complesso. Indipendentemente dalla divisione delle funzioni, i paraventi in legno si susseguono senza interruzione. Le sette ville furono divise in quattro suite private, un ristorante, una spa, una casa da tè, un night bar, punti d'incontro e spazi amministrativi.

"江南会" 该项目将7座传统风格的别墅改造成一座豪华会所。设计的思路是通过替换正面墙体从而创造出连贯性。重新设计的正面墙体使别墅的内部具有当代的空间特性,同时又不完全摒弃传统审美观。新的正面墙由一套层级系统组成,以达到控制温度,保护隐私及采光的目的。最外面一层需要超过700片木隔板错综复杂地组合而成。7幢别墅被分成四套私人套间,包括餐厅,按摩浴池,茶座,夜间酒吧,会议厅及行政区。木屏风的连续使用使得功能区的划分很合理。

THREE SHADOWS PHOTOGRAPHY ART CENTER

GALLERY | CAOCHANGDI, BEIJING, CHINA
Three Shadows Photography Art Center
Design date: 08–09.2006
Construction date: 09.2006–05.2007
Total built area: 2.000 m²

Built on a former auto repair shop, the Three Shadows Photography Art Center's zigzag layout conforms to its irregularly shaped site. It serves as an institution for the education, production and display of photography and video. The main structure and an enclosing wall define two triangular outdoor spaces, a separate building and three pavilions form the rest of the site. The garden space with its grass, trees, natural, rough-cut stones, and the simple and functional arrangement of the paths define the structure. The main building's façade is the most expressive part in the complex: several layers of brick compose a relief, added by an irregular pattern of scaffolding holes in the surface.

Auf dem Gelände einer ehemaligen Autowerkstatt errichtet, passt sich der zickzackförmige Grundriss des Three Shadows Photography Art Center der unregelmäßigen Grundstückform an. Das Zentrum dient als Ausbildungseinrichtung, zur Produktion und Ausstellung von Fotografie und Video. Das Hauptgebäude und eine Umgebungsmauer bilden zwei dreieckige Außenräume, ein gesonderter Bau und drei Pavillons den Rest des Geländes. Der bepflanzte Garten mit grob behauenen Steinen und die einfache und funktionelle Anordnung der Pfade definieren die Struktur. Die Fassade des Hauptgebäudes stellt den ausdrucksvollsten Komplexteil dar: Ein Relief aus mehreren Ziegelschichten mit einem unregelmäßigen Lochmuster in der Oberfläche.

Costruido a partir de lo que fue originalmente un taller mecánico de automóviles, la disposición en zig zag del Three Shadows Photography Art Center se adapta a la forma irregular del lugar y hace las veces de instituto para la enseñanza, la producción y la exposición de fotografías y vídeo. La estructura principal y un muro envolvente delinean dos espacios externos con forma triangular. Una construcción independiente y tres pabellones conforman el resto del lugar. El espacio del jardín con su prado, los árboles y las piedras naturales de corte basto, además de las soluciones para senderos sencillos y funcionales definen la estructura. La parte más emblemática del edificio principal la representa su fachada, sobre cuya superficie sobresale un relieve compuesto por varias capas de ladrillos resaltado además por un patrón irregular de huecos.

Erigé sur une ancienne usine de réparation de voitures, la disposition en zigzag du Three Shadows Photography Art Center s'adapte à la forme irrégulière du site et est maintenant utilisée comme institut pour l'enseignement, la production et l'exposition de photographies et vidéos. La structure principale et un mur d'enceinte dessinent deux espaces externes à la forme triangulaire. Un bâtiment séparé et trois pavillons forment le reste du site. L'espace du jardin avec sa pelouse, les arbres et les pierres naturelles à la coupe brute, ainsi que les solutions pour des chemins simples et fonctionnels, définissent la structure. La partie la plus emblématique de l'immeuble principal est représentée par sa façade, dont la surface est soulignée par un relief composé par plusieurs couches de briques mise en relief encore plus par un motif irrégulier de cavités à charpente.

Ricavato da una pre-esistente officina di riparazioni auto, la disposizione a zig zag del Three Shadows Photography Art Center si adatta alla forma irregolare del terreno. Il centro funge da istituto per l'insegnamento, la produzione e l'esposizione di fotografie e video. La struttura principale ed un muro di cinta delineano due spazi esterni di forma triangolare. Un edificio a parte e tre padiglioni formano il resto del sito. Lo spazio del giardino con il suo prato, gli alberi e le pietre naturali dal taglio grezzo, oltre alle soluzioni per sentieri semplici e funzionali definiscono la struttura. La parte più emblematica dell'edificio principale è rappresentata dalla sua facciata, sulla cui superficie spicca un rilievo composto da diversi strati di mattoni, messo ulteriormente in risalto da un motivo irregolare di cavità ad orditura.

"三影堂摄影艺术中心"是在一家旧汽车修理店的基础上建成的，其蜿蜒曲折的布局与不规则的地形相一致。该中心作为摄影和摄像的教学，创作及展示机构。主体建筑与一面围墙的结合划分出两块三角形室外区域。其余建筑包括一幢独立的建筑和三座展览厅。花园里的草，树木，自然景色，切割粗糙的石块以及布局简单却很有用的小径使该建筑独具风格。主体建筑的正面墙是这套综合建筑中最富有表现力的部分。几层砖块组成了一座浮雕，而这一效果由于和遗留在墙面上的脚手架孔组成的不规则图案而得到了加强。

241 CAOCHANGDI
GALLERIES AND STUDIOS
CAOCHANGDI, BEIJING, CHINA
Design date: 2007
Construction date: 2007
Total built area: 7.230 m²

The slightly irregular property consists of twelve square and seven rectangular plots for a total of nineteen galleries or artist studios. Ai Weiwei designed three different building sizes. All the units, except for three, consist of L-shaped structures with courtyards, bordered by the neighboring building. The rigid grid is transformed into an exciting space by irregular positioning of some of the units. Some L-shaped structures are rotated, opening up larger gardens and varying the qualities of the long perspectives through the site. Paths and alleys form semi public spaces, partitioned with wooden fences that reduce the starkness and severity of the complex of gray brick structures and gray brick paved pathways. The homogenous combination of gray brick and wood creates a bold statement in the creative village.

Das leicht unregelmäßige Gelände besteht aus zwölf quadratförmigen und sieben rechteckigen Baugrundstücken für insgesamt neunzehn Galerien oder Künstlerstudios. Ai Weiwei entwarf drei unterschiedlich große Bauten. Alle Einheiten, bis auf drei, sind L förmig angelegt und besitzen Innenhöfe, die durch die Nachbargebäude begrenzt sind. Das starre Raster wird durch die unregelmäßige Positionierung einiger Einheiten in einen spannenden Raum verwandelt. Manche der L-förmigen Gebäude sind gedreht, sodass sich die Gärten verbreitern und die langen Geländeperspektiven ändern. Pfade und Alleen bilden halböffentliche Räume, die durch Holzzäune unterteilt sind, die die Strenge und Schlichtheit der grauen Ziegelbauten und grau gepflasterten Pfade reduzieren. Die einheitliche Kombination von gleichfarbigem Ziegel und Holz behauptet sich auf kühne Weise im kreativen Dorf.

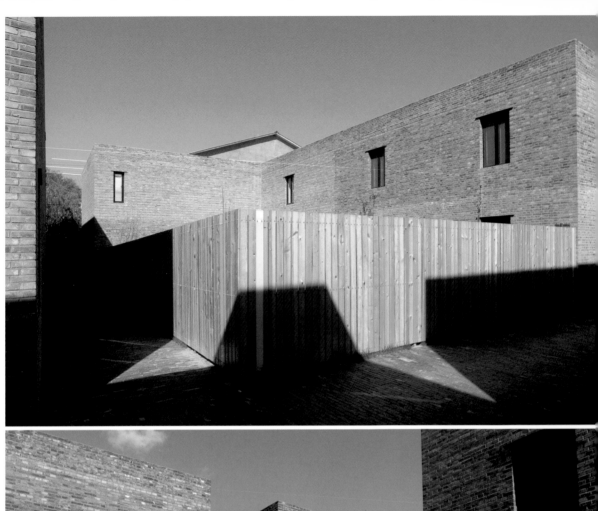

La propiedad, ligeramente irregular, se compone de doce parcelas cuadradas y siete rectangulares, haciendo un total de diecinueve entre galerías y estudios de arte. Ai Weiwei ha diseñado tres tamaños diferentes de edificio. Todas las unidades, con excepción de tres, están formadas por construcciones en forma de L con patio, colindantes con los edificios vecinos. El rígido esquema tramado se convierte en espacio emocional a través de la colocación irregular de algunas unidades. Algunas de las construcciones con forma de L están giradas, encerrando jardines más amplios, y variando así la cualidad de las largas perspectivas a través del lugar. Senderos y caminillos crean espacios semipúblicos, separados por medio de recintos de madera que reducen la austeridad y desnudez del conjunto de las construcciones y de los pasajes de ladrillo gris. De la combinación homogénea de madera y ladrillos grises nace una declaración audaz en el pueblo creativo.

La propriété, légèrement irrégulière, conçue de sept lots rectangulaires et douze carrés en formant au total dix-neuf galeries ou ateliers d'art. Ai Weiwei a réalisé des bâtiments de trois dimensions différentes. Toutes les unités sauf trois sont constituées par des constructions en forme de L avec cour qui confinent avec le bâtiment latéral. Le schéma rigid à grille devient un espace émotionnant grâce au positionnement irrégulier de quelques unités. Certaines constructions en forme de L sont tournées et dévoilent des jardins plus amples, en changeant donc la qualité des perspectives longues à travers le site. Des chemins et des ruelles créent des espaces semi-publics séparés par des clôtures en bois qui réduisent l'austérité et la nudité des constructions et des passages en briques gris. La combinaison homogène de bois et brique gris donne vie à une déclaration audacieuse dans le village créatif.

La proprietà, leggermente irregolare, si compone di dodici lotti quadrati e sette rettangolari, per un totale di dicianove tra gallerie o studi d'arte. Ai Weiwei ha progettato tre differenti misure d'edificio. Tutte le unità, ad eccezione di tre, sono costituite da costruzioni a forma di L con cortile, confinanti con l'edificio a fianco. Il rigido schema a griglia diventa spazio emozionante attraverso il posizionamento irregolare delle unità. Alcune delle costruzioni a forma di L sono ruotate, schiudendo giardini più ampi, e variando così la qualità delle prospettive lunghe attraverso il sito. Sentieri e vialetti creano spazi semi pubblici, separati per mezzo di recinzioni in legno che riducono l'austerità e la semplicità d'insieme delle costruzioni e dei passaggi in mattone grigio. Dalla combinazione omogenea del legno e dei mattoni grigi nasce una dichiarazione audace nel villaggio creativo.

"241 草场地"　这座稍显不规则的建筑群由1 2块方形和7块矩形分区组成，共17座画廊或艺术工作室。艾未未设计了3种不同建筑尺寸。所有单元，除了3处外，都是由L型建筑和院子组成，与邻近的建筑相接。生硬的方格由于某些单元的不规则布置而发生变化，产生激动人心的效果。通过旋转某些L型建筑获得面积更大的花园，从而改变整个区域远景视图的特性。小径和巷道营造出半公共的区域，用木栅栏隔开，缓和了整个建筑群由于灰砖结构与灰砖路带来的僵硬与严肃氛围。灰砖与木材的同质结合是关于创新性村庄的一次引人注目的宣言。

RED BRICK ART GALLERIES
GALLERIES AND STUDIOS
CAOCHANGDI, BEIJING, CHINA
Design date: 2007
Construction date: 2007
Total site area: 10.990 m²
Total built area: 6.120 m²

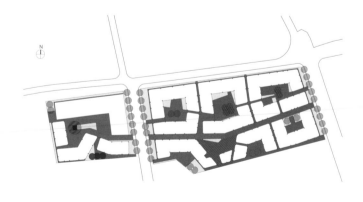

The complex contains twenty five galleries or artist studios and a dozen living units, organized around five courtyards and a central spine. The corridor is lined with approximately 10-meter-high walls of red bricks, red grout and red window frames, contained and reinforced by poured-in-place gray concrete beams and columns. The proportions of the four-meter-wide corridor and the 1.6-meter-wide secondary circulation in relationship to the walls give a severe and dramatic passage. The use of a prevalent urban form allows the project's elements, such as alleyways, to blend into neighboring sites. In this way the merely mono functional complex reproduces the traditional urban fabric of a village, where cars are banned and human scale dictates proportion and space. The red brick galleries are a departure from the gray brick structures that Ai Weiwei made popular in the Caochangdi area of Beijing.

Der Komplex besteht aus fünfundzwanzig Galerien oder Ateliers und einem Dutzend Wohneinheiten, die sich um fünf Höfe und eine zentrale Achse herum organisieren. Diesen Erschließungsgang säumen circa 10 Meter hohe Mauern, die mit rotem Ziegel, rotem Mörtel und roten Fensterrahmen versehen sind und durch graue vor Ort gegossene Betonbalken und Säulen verstärkt werden. Die Proportionen des 4 Meter breiten Gangs und des 1.6 Meter breiten sekundären Umlaufs schaffen in der Beziehung zu den Wänden einen strengen und dramatischen Durchgang. Der Gebrauch einer überwiegend städtischen Form erlaubt Elementen, wie zum Beispiel den Gassen, mit den benachbarten Grundstücken zu verschmelzen. Auf diese Weise bringt der rein monofunktionale Komplex den traditionellen städtischen Charakter eines Dorfes zum Vorschein, wo Autos verbannt sind und der menschliche Maßstab Proportion und Raum diktiert. Der rote Ziegelbau stellt eine Art Abschied von den grauen Ziegelstrukturen dar, die Ai Weiwei im Pekinger Caochangdi Viertel bekannt machten.

El complejo contiene veintecinco galerías o estudios de artistas y una docena de unidades habitables, organizadas alrededor de cinco patios y un eje central. El pasillo está flanqueado por una pared de unos 10 metros de altura hecha de ladrillo rojo, mortero rojo y ventanas con marcos rojos, contenidos y reforzados por vigas y columnas de hormigón gris realizados in situ. Las proporciones del corredor de 4 metros y de los pasajes secundarios de 1.6 metros en relación con la pared crean un pasaje austero y teatral. El empleo de formas sobre todo urbanas permite a los elementos del proyecto, como las callejuelas, mezclarse con los lugares de los alrededores. De esta manera el complejo meramente mono-funcional reproduce el tradicional tejido urbano de un pueblo, donde los automóviles están prohibidos y donde la medida humana dicta proporciones y espacio. Las galerías de ladrillo rojo marcan la partida de las estructuras de ladrillo gris por las que Ai Weiwei se hace popular en la zona Caochangdi en Pekín.

L'ensemble contient vingt-cinq galeries ou ateliers d'artistes et une douzaine de unités d'habitation organisées autour de cinq cours et une dorsale centrale. Le couloir est longé d'un mur en briques et mortier rouges d'environ 10 mètres de hauteur. Les montants rouges des fenêtres sont contenus et renforcés par poutres et colonnes en béton gris coulé sur place. Par rapport au mur, les proportions du couloir de 4 mètres de largeur et du passage secondaire de 1.6 mètres créent un passage austère et théâtral. L'emploi de formes essentiellement urbaines permet aux éléments du projet, tels que les ruelles, de se mêler aux lieux environnants. De cette façon l'ensemble purement mono-fonctionnel reproduit le traditionnel tissu urbain d'un village où les voitures sont interdites et la mesure humaine définit espaces et proportions. Les galeries en briques rouges représentent une dérogation aux structures en briques grises pour lesquelles Ai Weiwei devînt populaire dans la zone Caochangdi de Pékin.

Il complesso contiene venticinque gallerie o studi di artisti e una dozzina di unità abitative, organizzate intorno a cinque cortili ed ad una dorsale centrale. Il corridoio è fiancheggiato da un muro alto circa 10 metri in mattone rosso, malta rossa e da finestre dagli stipiti rossi, contenuti e rinforzati da travi e colonne in calcestruzzo grigio colati sul posto. Le proporzioni del corridoio largo quattro metri e del transito secondario di 1.6 metri in rapporto al muro creano un passaggio austero e teatrale. L'utilizzo di forme in prevalenza urbane permette agli elementi del progetto, quali i vicoli, di mescolarsi con i luoghi circostanti. In tal modo il complesso meramente monofunzionale riproduce il tradizionale tessuto urbano di un villaggio, dove le auto sono bandite e dove la scala umana detta proporzioni e spazio. Le gallerie in mattone rosso costituiscono una deviazione dalle strutture in mattone grigio per le quali Ai Weiwei divenne popolare nell'area Caochangdi di Pechino.

"红砖艺术画廊" 该套综合设施包括25座画廊和艺术工作室以及十几处起居单元，建筑布局围绕5座院子及一条建筑中轴线。走廊两边是近10米高的红砖墙，红色的水泥浆及红色的窗框，包括灰色的混凝土横梁及圆柱，而其位置恰到好处，建筑结构因此得到加强。4米宽的走廊以及基于墙壁设计的1.6米宽的徊廊之间的比例营造出朴素而富有戏剧性效果的通道。流行的都市造形的使用使得建筑的组成元素，例如小巷，与周围的环境融合到一起。如此一来，这套几乎是单一功能的综合建筑在农村重现了传统的都市结构，这里汽车遭到禁止，人支配着平衡与空间。红砖画廊摆脱了灰砖结构，这使艾未未在北京草场地变得受欢迎。

ARTFARM
GALLERY | SALT POINT, NEW YORK, USA
Cooperation with HHF architects
Design date: 08.2006 – 02.2007
Construction date: 03.2007 – 06.2008
Total built area: 383 m²

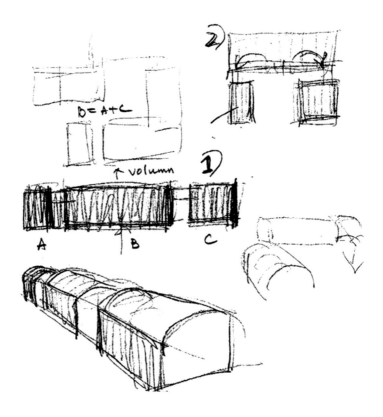

The Artfarm is located on the site of an existing private residence built in the 80's. It is designed as a gallery for an art collection. The building had to be big and low cost at the same time. The interior is subdivided into different sized showrooms and spaces designated to store art. The atmosphere is very soft due to the white upholstered PVC ceiling and creates a contrast with the metallic external building wrap. The outer shape is a result of the pre-fabricated and easy to assemble type of steel building, which often gets used for agricultural purposes in that area. With its abstract metallic appearance, the building becomes an equal member of a whole group of sculptures which are spread out in the landscape. The three volumes are put on a solid concrete slab which follows the existing grade of the site. The different levels are connected through a continuous cascading ramp through the building's central axis. This central hallway provides access to all spaces, allowing artwork to be exchanged easily between storage and showrooms and, works at the same time as a gallery.

Die Artfarm liegt auf dem Grundstück eines vorhandenen privaten Wohnsitzes aus den 80'er Jahren und ist als Galerie für eine Kunstsammlung bestimmt. Das Gebäude musste groß und gleichzeitig kostengünstig sein. Im Gebäudeinneren befinden sich unterschiedlich große Ausstellungs- und Aufbewahrungsräume für Kunst. Die Atmosphäre ist aufgrund der weißen, gepolsterten PVC-Decke sehr weich und schafft einen Kontrast zur metallischen Außenhülle. Die äußere Form ergibt sich aus dem vorgefertigten und leicht zusammen fügbaren Stahlbautypus, der in der Gegend häufig zu landwirtschaftlichen Zwecken eingesetzt wird. Mit seiner abstrakten metallischen Erscheinung reiht sich das Gebäude in eine Skulpturengruppe ein, die in der Landschaft verstreut ist. Die drei Volumina stehen auf einer festen Betonplatte, die dem Geländeverlauf folgt. Die unterschiedlichen Ebenen sind durch eine gleichmäßig fallende Rampe entlang der Gebäudehauptachse miteinander verbunden. Dieser Hauptgang erschließt alle Räume, ermöglicht, dass die Kunstwerke leicht zwischen dem Lager und den Ausstellungsräumen transportiert werden können und dient gleichzeitig als Galerie.

La Artfarm se sitúa en el terreno de una residencia privada ya existente construida en los años ochenta y diseñada como galería para una colección de arte. El edificio tenía que ser al mismo tiempo grande y de bajo coste. El interior está dividido en espacios de exposición de diferente tamaño y en espacios destinados al depósito de obras de arte. El ambiente resulta muy suave gracias al techo tapizado con PVC blanco que crea un contraste con la envolvente metálica exterior. La forma externa deriva de la típica construcción de acero prefabricada, fácil de montar, y que a menudo se emplea en esa zona con función agrícola. Con su aspecto metálico abstracto, la estructura se convierte ella misma en parte de un grupo de esculturas, diseminadas en el paisaje de alrededor. Los tres edificios están situados sobre una plancha de hormigón macizo que se adapta a la pendiente ya existente. Los diferentes niveles están unidos entre ellos mediante una rampa inclinada a lo largo del eje central de la construcción. Este corredor ofrece acceso a todos los espacios, permitiendo el cambio fácil de las obras de arte entre el depósito y las salas de exposición, a la vez que funciona como galería.

L'Artfarm se situe sur le site d'une résidence privée pré-existante bâtie aux années '80 et elle est conçue comme une galerie pour une collection d'art. L'immeuble devait être grand et à bas coût en même temps. À l'intérieur il est subdivisé en espaces d'exposition de dimensions différentes et en espaces destinés au dépôt d'œuvres d'art. L'atmosphère est très diffuse grâce à la présence d'un plafond revêtu en PVC blanc matelassé qui crée un contraste avec le revêtement externe en métal. La forme à l'extérieur dérive de la typique construction en acier préfabriquée, facile à assembler et utilisée souvent dans cette zone dans le secteur agricole. Avec son aspect métallique abstrait, la structure devient elle même partie d'un groupe de sculptures disséminées dans le paysage environnant. Les trois bâtiments sont positionnés sur une plaque en béton massif à travers une rampe inclinée le long de l'axe centrale de la construction. Ce couloir permet d'accéder à tous les espaces, en permettant un échange facile des pièces d'art entre dépôt et salles d'exposition et en servant en même temps de galerie.

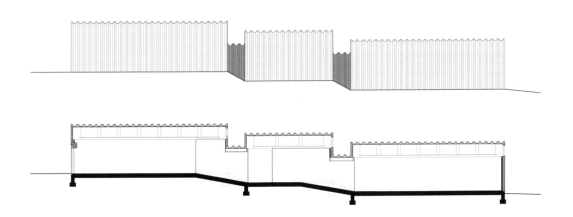

L' Artfarm si colloca sul terreno di una preesistente residenza privata costruita negli anni Ottanta ed è progettata come una galleria per una collezione d'arte. L'edificio doveva essere allo stesso tempo grande e a basso costo. L'interno è suddiviso in spazi espositivi di diversa misura e in spazi destinati al deposito di opere d'arte. L'atmosfera risulta molto soffice grazie al soffitto rivestito e tappezzato in PVC bianco che crea contrasto con il rivestimento esterno in metallo. La struttura esterna deriva dalla tipica costruzione in acciaio prefabbricato, facilmente assemblabile, che spesso è utilizzata in quell'area a scopo agricolo. Con il suo astratto aspetto metallico, l'edificio diviene esso stesso parte di un gruppo di sculture, disseminate nel paesaggio circostante. I tre volumi sono posti su di una lastra di calcestruzzo massiccio che asseconda la pendenza del luogo. I diversi livelli sono collegati per mezzo di una rampa inclinata lungo l'asse centrale dell'edificio. Questo corridoio permettere di accedere a tutti gli spazi, consentendo un facile scambio dei pezzi d'arte tra deposito e sale espositive e fungendo contemporaneamente da galleria.

"艺术农场"建于一处80年代的私人住宅区，设计成专业的艺术收藏画廊。设计必须同时满足大型建筑和低成本的要求。内部被再次分划成不同尺寸的展览区及艺术品存放区。顶部经过装饰的PVC天花板营造出非常柔和的氛围，与外部的金属覆盖形成对比。外部形状得益于经过预制且易于组合的钢材，而这一材料在该地区通常用于农业。由于其抽象的金属外形，该结构也成为分布在该风景区内雕塑群中的一员。三座建筑建于坚固的混凝土板之上，而混凝土板则按照原有的地面层级布置。沿着建筑中轴线砌成的连续层叠斜坡将各层联接起来。沿着中间的走廊可以到达所有的区域，这使得艺术品可以在储藏室与展览区之间自由调换，而同时发挥画廊的作用。

TSAI RESIDENCE
RESIDENCE | ANCRAM, NEW YORK, USA
Cooperation with HHF architects
Design date: 05.2005 – 02.2006
Construction date: 03.2006 – 08.2008
Total floor area: 375 m²

The Tsai Residence is a country house designed for two young art collectors. The design reflects their request for a simple, abstract looking piece, sitting almost without scale on top of the site. The building is a typical American balloon frame construction and divided into a series of four equal sized boxes. It is elegant and slightly forbidding on the outside but expansive and light-filled on the inside. The boxes are built as simple wood construction covered with corrugated metal panels on the outside and wood and gypsum panels on the inside. The floor plan is based on the needs of a traditional country house. The organization of the rooms is only partially a direct consequence of the rigid outer form. The room sequence reflects the idea of a private gallery. The living room focuses on the different light conditions needed for an existing and future art collection, while the great view into the nearby countryside is present without being dominant. Natural light is coming into the spaces through the openings in between the outer boxes.

Die Tsai Residenz war als Landhaus für zwei junge Kunstsammler erdacht, deren Wunsch ein einfacher, abstrakt wirkender Bau war, der beinahe maßstabslos oben auf dem Gelände sitzt. Das Gebäude ist nach dem Muster der typisch amerikanischen *ballon frame construction* als Holzständerbau errichtet und gliedert sich in vier gleichgroße Boxen. Es ist elegant und gibt sich nach außen verschlossen, ist innen jedoch mitteilsam und sehr hell. Die einfache Holzkonstruktion ist außen mit Wellblech und innen mit Holz- und Gipstafeln verkleidet. Der Grundriss beruht auf den Bedürfnissen eines traditionellen Landhauses. Die Raumorganisation ist nur teilweise eine direkte Folge der starren Außenform und spiegelt die Idee von einer privaten Galerie wieder. Das Wohnzimmer konzentriert sich auf die unterschiedlichen Lichtverhältnisse, die die vorhandene und künftige Kunstsammlung erfordert, während der großartige Ausblick auf die Landschaft präsent aber nicht dominant ist. Natürliches Licht tritt durch die Öffnungen zwischen den Außenkästen in die Räume ein.

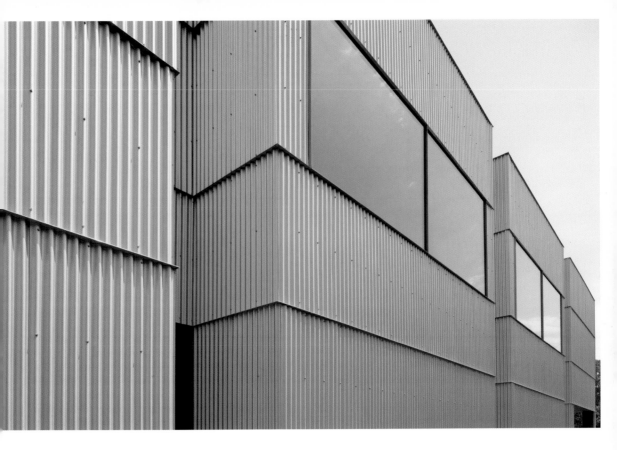

La Tsai Residence es una casa de campo ideada para dos jóvenes coleccionistas de arte. El diseño refleja su deseo de una obra sencilla y de aparencia abstracta, que se posa casi sin escala en el lugar. El edificio es una clásica construcción americana *balloon frame* dividida en una serie de cuatro cajas de dimensiones iguales. Elegante y ligeramente austera en el exterior, la obra se convierte en amplia y luminosa en el interior. Las cajas están construidas como sencillas costrucciones de madera recubiertas con paneles de metal ondulado en el exterior y paneles de yeso y madera en el interior. El plano de planta responde a las necesidades de una casa de campo tradicional. La organización del espacio es en parte consecuencia directa de la rigidez de la forma externa. La continuidad de las diferentes salas refleja la idea de una galería privada. La sala de estar se concibe sobre la base de las diferentes condiciones de luz necesarias en las colecciones de arte actuales y futuras mientras que la amplia visual sobre el campo que lo rodea está presente sin ser dominante. La luz natural inunda el espacio a través de las aberturas entre una caja y otra.

La Tsai Residence est une résidence de campagne réalisée pour deux jeunes amateurs d'art. Le projet reflète leur désir d'une œuvre simple et apparemment abstraite qui se situe sur le sommet du terrain sans référence d'échelle. Le bâtiment est une construction américaine classique *balloon frame* divisée en quatre boites de la même dimension. Élégante et légèrement austère à l'extérieur, l'œuvre devient ample et lumineuse à l'intérieur. Les boites sont des simples bâtiments en bois recouverts avec des panneaux en métal ondulés à l'extérieur et des panneaux en plâtre et bois à l'intérieur. Le plan des étages répond aux besoins d'une maison de campagne traditionnelle. L'organisation des espaces est seulement en partie une conséquence directe de la forme rigide externe. La succession des salles différentes reflète l'idée d'une galerie privée. Le séjour est conçu pour se focaliser sur les différentes conditions d'éclairage nécessaires aux collections d'art actuelles et futures, tandis que l'ample vue sur la campagne environnante est présente mais pas dominante. La lumière naturelle inonde l'espace à travers les ouvertures entre une boîte et l'autre.

La Tsai Residence è una residenza di campagna ideata per due giovani collezionisti d'arte. Il progetto riflette il loro desiderio di un'opera semplice ed astratta, che si collochi sulla sommità del sito quasi senza riferimento di scala. L'edificio è una classica costruzione americana *balloon frame* divisa quattro scatole di uguale dimensione. Elegante e leggermente austera all'esterno, l'opera si presenta ampia e luminosa all'interno. Le scatole sono semplici fabbricati in legno, ricoperti con pannelli in metallo ondulato all'esterno e pannelli in gesso e legno all'interno. La pianta risponde alle necessità di una tradizionale casa di campagna. L'organizzazione degli spazi è solo in parte diretta conseguenza della rigida forma esterna. Il susseguirsi dei diversi spazi riflette l'idea di una galleria privata. Il soggiorno si focalizza sulle diverse condizioni di luce necessarie alle collezioni d'arte attuali e future mentre l'ampia visuale sulla campagna circostante è presente senza essere dominante. La luce naturale inonda lo spazio attraverso le aperture tra una scatola e l'altra.

"蔡宅" 蔡宅是为两位艺术收藏家设计的乡村住宅。一件外形简单抽象的物体竖立在建筑位置的顶部，周围没有物体遮挡视线，这是他们的要求。该建筑为传统的美国轻快结构建筑，分成四个尺寸相同的厢房。其外形雅致却有些生硬，但内部宽敞且光线充足。厢房的建筑使用了简单的木板，外部覆盖了波浪形金属板，而内部则为木板及石膏板。地板的设计则是基于传统的农村住宅需求。外部生硬的造型对于内部的结构的影响很有限。生活区的设计重点考虑了现有及将来的艺术藏品对不同光线的需求，虽然观看周围乡村风景的视角很好，但其并不占据主体地位。不同房间的顺序反映了私人画廊的理念。自然光经过外部厢房之间的开口进入内部。

ORDOS 100
MASTERPLAN | ORDOS, INNER MONGOLIA, CHINA
Consulting on architects selection: Herzog & de Meuron
Masterplan design date: 01.2008
Total site area: 219.589 m²

The scope of the project was to develop one hundred villas in Ordos, Inner Mongolia. Ai Weiwei and FAKE Design developed the master plan for the one hundred parcels of land and curated the project, while the Swiss architectural firm Herzog & de Meuron proposed the one hundred participating architects from twenty seven countries who had to design a 1.000 m² villa.

Einhundert Villen sollen in Ordos, der Inneren Mongolei entstehen. Ai Weiwei und FAKE Design entwickelten den Master Plan für die einhundert Parzellen und waren für das Projekt verantwortlich, während die Schweizer Architekten Herzog & de Meuron die einhundert Architekten aus siebenundzwanzig Ländern vorschlugen, die die 1.000 m² großen Villen entwerfen sollen.

La finalidad de este proyecto era desarrollar cien casas de campo en Ordos, en Mongolia Interior. Ai Weiwei y Fake Design desarrollaron el plan piloto para cien parcelas de terreno y el estudio suizo de arquitectura Herzog & de Meuron se ocupó de sugerir a los cien arquitectos participantes originarios de veintisiete países que habrían de diseñar una casa de campo de 1.000 m².

Le but du projet était la construction de cent maisons à Ordos, dans la Mongolie interne. Ai Weiwei et Fake Design collaborèrent à la création et au développement du projet pilote concernant les cent lots de terrain, tandis que le bureau suisse d'architecture Herzog & de Meuron a suggéré des cent architectes provenant de vingt-sept pays différents, chargés du projet d'une maison de 1.000 m².

Lo scopo del progetto era la realizzazione di cento ville ad Ordos, nella Mongolia Interna. Ai Weiwei e Fake Design collaborarono alla creazione e allo sviluppo del progetto pilota relativo ai cento lotti di terreno, mentre lo studio svizzero d'architettura Herzog & de Meuron proposero i cento architetti provenienti da ventisette diversi paesi, incaricati a progettare una villa di 1.000 m².

"鄂尔多斯100号" 该项目的目标是在内蒙古鄂尔多斯建造100套别墅。艾未未与Fake Design为一百块地皮制定出总体设计，并协助这项工程，瑞士建筑公司赫尔佐格与德·穆龙挑选来自27个国家的100名设计师参与这项工程，他们自己也要设计一套1,000平方米的别墅。

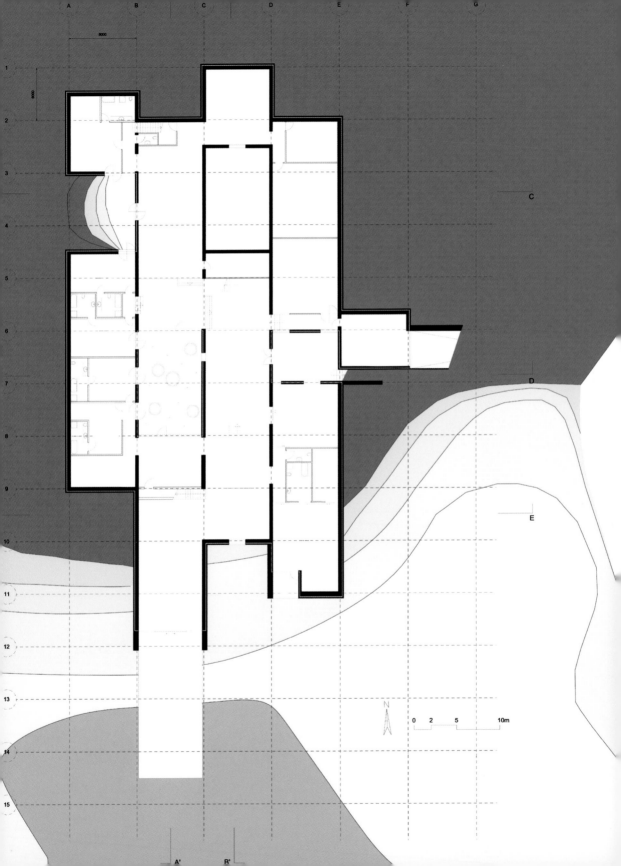

UNDERCOVER VILLA
RESIDENCE
ORDOS, INNER MONGOLIA, CHINA
Design date: 03 – 09.2007
Construction date: 09.2008 – present
Total area: 2.000 m²

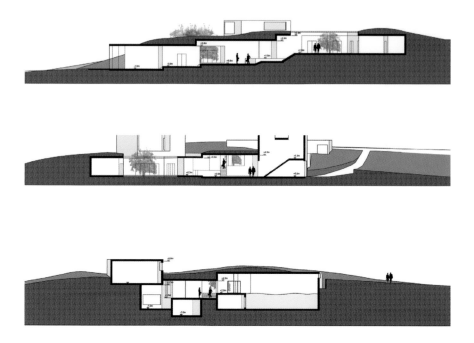

The Undercover Villa is part of a series of seven projects that began the development of a peninsula of sand dunes that would later be used for the Ordos 100 project. In order to be ecologically sensitive to the site and to the grass and sand formations of the Inner Mongolian plane, most of the building was submerged, while its site lines to the adjacent reservoir were maintained. By submerging the volume, the villa fits into the landscape without visually destroying the natural site. By pulling apart the structures on a north-south axis, the extrusions allow views to the surrounding landscape and the voids bring light to the interior. The extrusions and voids, combined with the sloping site, create varying conditions of interaction between the natural surroundings and the built form.

Die Undercover Villa ist Teil von sieben Projekten, die den Anfang der Entwicklung einer Halbinsel aus Sanddünen bilden, die später für das Ordos 100 Projekt Verwendung finden sollte. Um ökologisch sensibel auf die Landschaft, das Gras und die Sandformationen der Inneren Mongolischen Ebene zu reagieren, wurde das Gebäude größtenteils eingegraben und durch das angrenzende Wasserreservoir natürlich begrenzt. Das eingegrabene Haus fügt sich in die Landschaft ein, ohne die Natur visuell zu zerstören. Durch die Trennung der Baukörper auf der Nord-Südachse ergeben sich Ausblicke in die Umgebung und die leeren Zwischenräume bringen Licht ins Gebäudeinnere. Die herausstehenden Gebäudeteile und leeren Zwischenräume erzeugen in Kombination mit dem abfallenden Gelände unterschiedliche Wechselwirkungen zwischen der natürlichen Umgebung und der gebauten Form.

La Undercover Villa forma parte de una serie de siete proyectos que marcaron el inicio del desarrollo de una península de dunas arenosas que posteriormente sería utlizada para el proyecto Ordos 100. Con la intensión de manifestarse ecológicamente sensible al lugar y a las formaciones de hierba y arena de la llanura interior de Mongolia, la mayor parte del edificio fue enterrado manteniendo sus límites naturales con el estanque adyacente. De este modo, enterrando la estructura, la casa de campo se integra al paisaje sin destruir visualmente la naturaleza del lugar. Separando las construcciones según un eje norte-sur, las extrusiones permiten la vista del paisaje de alrededor mientras que los espacios vacíos introducen luz al interior. Las extrusiones y los vacíos, combinados con la inclinación del lugar, crean condiciones variables de interacción entre el entorno natural y la forma construida.

La Undercover Villa fait partie d'une série de sept projets qui ont marqué le début du développement d'une presqu'île de dunes sableuses qui ont été utilisées après pour le projet Ordos 100. Afin de s'adapter de façon écologique au lieu et créer une affinité avec les étendues herbues et les formations sableuses de la plaine interne de la Mongolie, la plupart du bâtiment a été enterré en gardant ses confines naturels avec le reservoir adjacent. De cette façon, en enterrant la structure, la maison s'insère dans le paysage sans détruire visuellement l'authenticité du lieu. En séparant les constructions selon un axe nord-sud, les extrusions permettent la vue du paysage entourant tandis que les espaces vides portent de la lumière à l'intérieur. Les extrusions et les vides, avec la pente du site, créent des conditions variables d'interaction entre environnement naturel et forme bâtie.

La Undercover Villa è parte della serie di sette progetti che segnarono l'inizio dello sviluppo di una penisola di dune sabbiose che sarebbero state in seguito utilizzate per il progetto Ordos 100. Per rispondere in modo ecologico all'ambiente circostante e creare affinità con le distese erbose e formazioni sabbiose della pianura interna della Mongolia, la maggior parte dell'edificio fu interrato mantenendo però, i suoi confini naturali con il lago adiacente. Sotterrando la struttura, la villa si inserisce nel paesaggio senza distruggere visivamente la naturalezza del luogo. Separando le costruzioni secondo un asse nord-sud, le estrusioni permettono la vista del paesaggio circostante e gli spazi vuoti portano luce all'interno. Le estrusioni ed i vuoti, combinati con la pendenza del terreno, creano condizioni variabili di interazione fra l'ambiente naturale e la forma costruita.

"秘密别墅"是一系列7套工程中的一项，是为开发沙丘半岛从而实施"鄂尔多斯100号"项目的始建工程。由于对地形敏感以及与内蒙古草地与沙漠地貌发生的联系，大多数建筑都是埋入式的，但并未阻碍观赏附近湖泊的视线。通过埋入式的布局，别墅融入到周围的风景之中，在视觉上没有破坏自然景观。建筑群分布在一条南北向的中轴线两旁，在建筑的突出部分可获得观赏周围风景的视角，而自然光从气孔进入建筑内部。建筑的突出部分和气孔以及倾斜的地表，使得自然环境与建筑之间的相互作用不断变化。

THE DOG HOUSE
RESIDENTIAL BUILDING | TOKYO, JAPAN
Design date: 08–09.2008
Total floor area: 182 m²

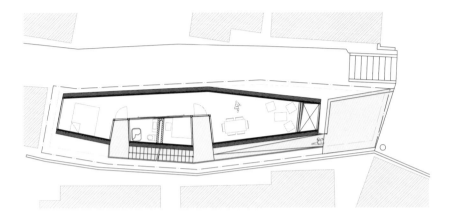

As a response to the restrictions and regulations that govern building design in Tokyo, the Dog House began with an extrusion of the allowable footprint and letting the limitations become the means by which the maximum allowable volume could be carved out. The glazing of the building got treated with a graphic of the client's dog. The displayed graphic give the impression of a giant dog, housed within the structure. In addition to the client's home, the architects were asked to redesign the client's Mercedes G-Wagon. Responding to the man and the dog, the car became a blueprint, expressing the dog on the truck's exterior.

Als Reaktion auf die Beschränkungen und Regulierungen, die das Baugeschehen in Tokyo bestimmen, konzentrierte sich der Dog House Entwurf auf die Erweiterung der zulässigen Bebauungsfläche und ließ somit die Begrenzung zum Mittel werden, um das maximal vorgesehene Volumen zu erreichen. Die Gebäudeverglasung wurde mit einer Grafik des Hundes des Kunden versehen, welche den Eindruck vermittelt, als ob ein riesiger Hund die Struktur bewohnt. Die Architekten sollten zusätzlich zum Haus auch den Wagen des Kunden, einen Mercedes G-Wagon neu entwerfen. Mit Rücksicht auf den Kunden und seinen Hund, wurde das Auto ebenfalls zu einer Blaupause, die den Hund auf dem Wagenäußeren darstellt.

Como respuesta a las reglas y restricciones que rigen el diseño edilicio en Tokyo, la Dog House comenzó con una ampliación de la planta permitida e haciendo que las restricciones se convirtieran en el instrumento mediante el cual obtener el máximo de la volumetría prevista. Los ventanales del edificio fueron intervenidos con una gráfica inspirada en el perro del cliente. Tal gráfica hacen referencia directa al cuerpo del perro, dando la impresión que el interior aloja un perro gigantesco. Además de la casa del cliente, a los arquitectos se les pidió diseñar de nuevo su Mercedes G-Wagon. En contemporanea consideración del hombre, del perro y del coche, la G-Wagon se convirtió en una cianografía que representaba al perro en el exterior del auto.

En réponse aux règles et aux limitations qui dirigent le design du bâtiment à Tokyo, la Dog House commença par l'agrandissement du plan approuvé et transforma les limitations en un outil pour obtenir le maximum de la volumétrie prévue. Les baies vitrées de l'immeuble furent réalisées avec une représentation graphique qui s'inspirait au chien du client. Les parties qui montrent ce graphisme se rapportent directement au corps du chien, en donnant l'impression que les intérieurs hébergent un chien gigantesque. Outre la maison du client, on demanda aux architectes de redessiner sa Mercedes G-Wagon. En considérant l'homme et le chien, la voiture devînt une cyanotypie qui représentait aussi le chien à l'extérieur du camion.

In risposta alle regole e restrizioni che determinano l'edilizia a Tokyo, la Dog House cominciò con un ampliamento della pianta consentita e fece si che le limitazioni divenissero lo strumento per mezzo del quale ottenere il massimo della volumetria prevista. Le vetrate dell'edificio furono realizzate con una grafica ispirata al cane del cliente. Tale grafica fa riferimento diretto al corpo del cane, dando l'impressione che l'interno ospiti un cane gigantesco. Oltre alla casa del cliente, agli architetti fu chiesto di ridisegnare la sua Mercedes G-Wagon. In contemporanea considerazione dell'uomo e del cane, l'auto divenne una cianografia che raffigurava il cane sull'esterno dell'autocarro.

"狗舍" 由于东京建筑设计规范的限制与法规, 狗舍以允许的最大突出空间开始, 使法律限制 获得了最大空间。狗舍的玻璃上贴着来自于客户的狗的图片。狗舍展览图片的部分直接与狗的体形联系起来, 给人的印象是狗舍里有只巨大的狗。除了客户的家, 建筑师还被要求重新设计客户的梅赛德斯G系列越野车。作为对客户, 狗, 赛车的回应, G系列越野车成为设计蓝图, 拖车外部贴上了狗的标志。

NATIONAL STADIUM
SPORTS ARENA | BEIJING, CHINA
Cooperation with Herzog & de Meuron
Design date (Stadium): 01.2002 – 03.2004
Construction date: 2004 – 2008
Total built area: 77.670 m² | Total site area: 298.000 m²
Design date (Landscape): 11.2003 – 03.2004

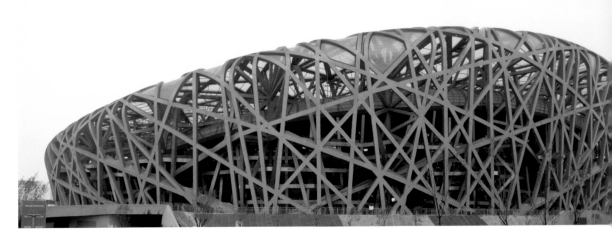

The Olympic National Stadium, widely known as "the bird's nest" due to its striking, seemingly random weave of raked steel girders became an international icon during the 2008 Olympics. The structure is the result of a collaborative conceptualization between the Swiss architecture firm Herzog & de Meuron and Ai Weiwei. The artist encouraged the architects to create a "crazy chaotic structure", providing sketches of a tree and other classical Chinese poetic images to illustrate the idea of order versus disorder. The Stadium is situated on a gentle rise in the center of the Olympic complex to the north of Beijing. It is conceived as a large collective vessel. The grid of the load-bearing structure encases the building, but also appears to penetrate it. The components look like a thicket of supports, beams and stairs, almost like an artificial forest. This Piranesian space surrounding the interior of the stadium represents façade, structure, decoration and public space all in one. It is the link between the city outside and the interior of the stadium and is, at the same time, an autonomous, urban site. This area between inside and outside affords the opportunity to create a new kind of urban and public place.

Das Olympische Nationalstadion, aufgrund seines auffallenden, scheinbar zufälligen Netzes aus Stahltragbalken, in aller Welt als „Vogelnest" bekannt, wurde durch die Olympischen Spiele 2008 zu einer internationalen Ikone. Das Konzept der Struktur entstand in einer Zusammenarbeit mit dem Schweizer Büro Herzog & de Meuron. Ai Weiwei ermutigte die Architekten zu einer „verrückten chaotischen Struktur" und veranschaulichte mit Hilfe von Baumskizzen und klassischen chinesischen Zeichnungen die Idee von Ordnung versus Unordnung. Das Stadion liegt auf einer leichten Erhöhung im Zentrum des Olympischen Komplexes in Pekings Norden und präsentiert sich als großes, kollektives Gefäß. Die Gitterstruktur des Tragwerks umhüllt den Baukörper nicht nur, sie durchdringt ihn gleichsam. Wie in einem künstlichen Wald formen die einzelnen Bestandteile ein Dickicht von Stützen, Balken, Fassadenelementen und Treppen. Dieser piranesische Raum umgibt das Stadioninnere, stellt gleichzeitig Hülle, Struktur, Ornament und öffentlichen Raum dar. Er verbindet den Außenraum der Stadt mit dem Innenraum des Stadiums und ist zugleich ein autonomer, urbaner Ort. Ein Zwischenraum, der einen neuartigen, urbanen und öffentlichen Ort ermöglicht.

El Estadio Olímpico Nacional, conocido comúnmente como "nido de pájaro", debida a su sorprendente y evidentemente casual tejido de vigas de acero entrelazadas, se convertió en un icono internacional durante las Olimpiadas de 2008. Su estructura es el resultado de la conzeptualización en equipo entre el estudio Herzog & de Meuron y Ai Weiwei. El artista animó a los arquitectos a crear "una estructura locamente caótica", para la que él mismo les dio un boceto inicial de un árbol y otras imágenes poéticas clásicas chinas que ilustrasen la idea de orden en contraposición al caos. El Estadio está situado sobre una ligera pendiente en el centro del complejo olímpico hacia el norte de Pekín y ha sido concebido como un gran contenedor colectivo. El enbramado de la estructura autoportante constituye la edificación a la vez que parece penetrarla. Los componentes forman una intrincada malla de apoyos, vigas y escaleras que parecen una jungla artificial. Este espacio Piranesiano rodea todo el interior del estadio, su fachada, su estructura, sus ornamentos y la zona pública conforman una única estructura. Es esta estructura lo que constituye una unión entre la ciudad y el interior del estadio, y ofrece, al mismo tiempo, un entorno urbano independiente dando vida a una nueva idea de lugar público urbano.

Le Stade Olympique National, communément connu sous le nom de « Nid d'Oiseau », est devenu une icône internationale pendant les Jeux Olympiques de 2008. Cette structure en poutres d'acier entrelacées, de fort impact et apparament casuelle, est née de la collaboration entre le bureau Herzog & de Meuron et Ai Weiwei. L'artiste encouragea les architectes à créer « une structure follement chaotique », en fournissant lui même des ébauches d'un arbre et d'autres images poétiques classiques chinoises qui devaient illustrer l'idée d'ordre contre désordre. Le stade est situé sur une légère pente au milieu de l'ensemble olympique au nord de Pékin et il a été conçu comme un grand conteneur collectif. La grille della structure portante enrobe la construction et, en même temps, semble la pénétrer. Les composants ressemblent à un enchevêtrement de supports, poutres et escaliers, comme une forêt artificielle. Cet espace piranésien enferme l'intérieur du stade en constitue également sa façade, la structure, les décorations et la zone publique. L'intérieur représente le lien entre la ville et l'intérieur du stade, en restant, en même temps, une zone urbaine indépendante et en donnant vie à une nouvelle typologie de lieu public et urbain.

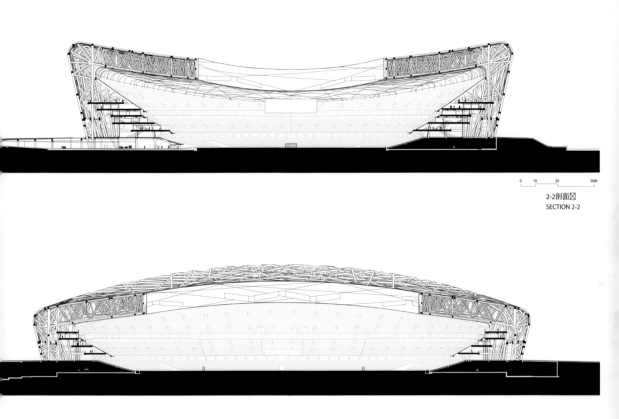

Lo Stadio Olimpico Nazionale, comunemente noto come "nido d'uccello" grazie al suo vistoso ed aparentamente casuale intreccio di travi d'acciaio, è diventato un'icona internazionale durante le Olimpiadi del 2008. La struttura è il risultato della collaborazione tra lo studio Herzog & de Meuron ed Ai Weiwei. L'artista incoraggiò gli architetti a creare "una struttura follemente caotica", fornendo lui stesso schizzi di un albero e altre immagini poetiche classiche cinesi che illustrassero l'idea di ordine contro disordine. Lo stadio è situato su di un lieve pendio al centro del complesso olimpico al nord di Pechino ed è stato concepito come un grande contenitore collettivo. La griglia della struttura portante racchiude l'edificio e, allo stesso tempo, sembra quasi penetrarlo. I componenti formano come in una foresta artificiale un'intricato di sostegni, travi e scale. Questo spazio piranesiano circonda l'interno dello stadio, costituisce allo stesso tempo la sua facciata, la struttura, le decorazioni e la zona pubblica e crea il legame tra la città e l'interno dello stadio, rimanendo, al contempo, un'area urbana indipendente che da vita ad una nuova tipologia di luogo pubblico ed urbano.

"国家体育馆" 奥林匹克国家体育馆因倾斜的钢梁看似随意的组合而被广泛称为 "鸟巢" ，注定要在2008年奥运会期间成为世界性标志。该结构是瑞士建筑设计公司的赫尔佐格和德·穆龙与艾未未合作设计的结果。后者鼓励建筑师创造出一座 "疯狂混乱的结构" ，并提供树木及其它中国诗歌意象的素描来说明规则与混乱之间的关系。体育馆建于北京市城北奥运会综合建筑群中心缓缓上升的斜坡上。它被设想成一座大型的容器集合体。承重网格包裹住建筑，但看上去又像是要透过建筑。主体看上去像是由支撑钢材，横梁与楼梯组成的丛林，几乎是一座人工森林。皮拉内西式空间环绕着体育馆的内部空间，融合体育馆外观，结构，装饰与公共区域为一体。它将外部城市与内部体育馆连接起来，同时又是独立的城市建筑。内部与外部之间的区域为创造新型城市及公共区域提供了可能。

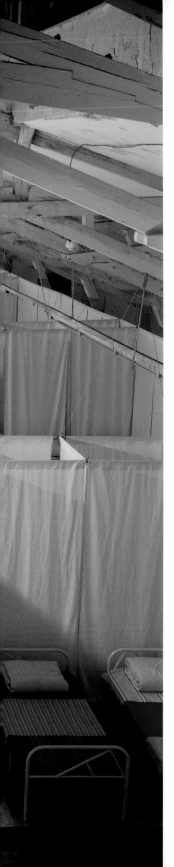

FAIRYTALE 1001
TEMPORARY DORMITORY
DOCUMENTA 12
KASSEL, GERMANY
Design date: 2007
Construction date: 2007
Total floor area: 2.000 m²

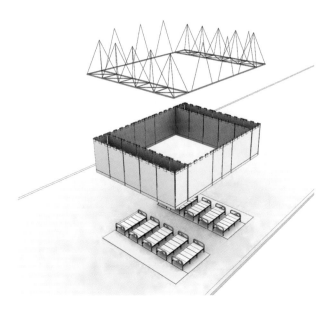

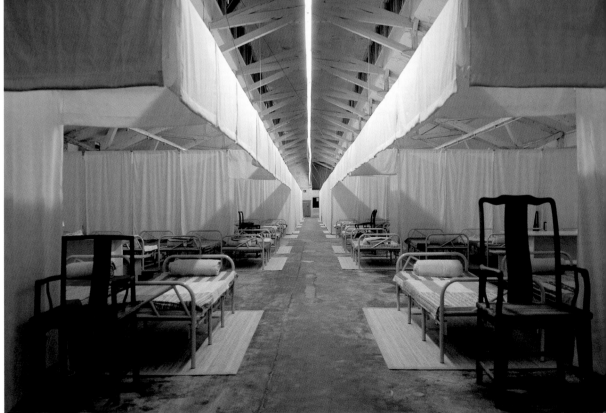

As part of his "Fairytale 1001" artwork for the documenta 12, Ai Weiwei sent 1001 Chinese to Kassel, Germany in the summer of 2007. In order to house them, he adapted a tent factory space to a dormitory. The adaptation was done through the installation of a suspended partition system. Using a light frame steel system in combination with fabric curtains, he provided private zones for sleeping and changing clothes. Woven bamboo mats were put on the floors and foldable cots stood next to each participant's associated Chinese Ming or Qing dynasty chair. The project can be deemed a social experiment to alter perception, increase awareness, and to disseminate information. The enlightenment of the individual is a theme that runs throughout Ai Weiwei's artwork and architecture.

Als Teil seines Kunstprojekts „Fairytale 1001" für die documenta 12 schickte Ai Weiwei 1001 Chinesen im Sommer 2007 nach Kassel. Um sie unterzubringen, wandelte er den Raum einer Zeltfabrik in einen Schlafsaal um. Hierfür verwendete er eine hängende Unterteilung. Die Kombination einer leichten Rahmenstahlkonstruktion und Stoffvorhängen schaffte private Zonen zum Schlafen und Umkleiden. Gewebte Bambusmatten wurden auf dem Fußboden verteilt und Klappbetten standen den Teilnehmern, neben Stühlen aus der chinesischen Ming oder Qing Dynastie, zur Verfügung. Das Projekt gleicht einem sozialen Experiment, das die Wahrnehmung verändert, das Bewusstsein verstärkt und Information verbreitet. Die Aufklärung des Individuums ist ständiges Thema in Ai Weiwei's Kunstwerken und seinen Bauten.

Como parte de la obra de arte "Fairytale 1001" para documenta 12, en el verano del 2007 Ai Weiwei envió 1001 ciudadanos chinos a Kassel, en Alemania. Para alojarles, adaptó como dormitorios los espacios de una fábrica de toldos instalando un sistema de paredes divisorias suspendidas. Empleando un sistema de armazón ligero de acero combinado con cortinas de tela, creó zonas reservadas para dormir y para vestuarios. En el suelo fueron colocadas esterillas de bambú entrelazado y, junto a cada participante, fueron puestas una cama plegable y una silla de la dinastía china Ming o Qing. El proyecto puede entenderse como un experimento social que tiene como finalidad alterar la percepción, desarrollar la toma de conciencia y divulgar información. La iluminación del individuo es un tema que se trasmite a través del arte y la arquitectura de Ai Weiwei.

Dans le cadre de l'œuvre d'art « Fairytale 1001 » pour documenta 12, pendant l'été 2007 Ai Weiwei envoya 1001 citoyens chinois à Kassel, en Allemagne. Afin de les accueillir, il transforma en dortoir les espaces d'une manufacture de rideaux en installant un système de cloisons suspendues. Grâce à l'emploi d'un système de châssis légers en acier et de rideaux en tissu, il créa des zones dédiées au coucher utilisables aussi comme vestiaires. Le sol fut revêtu avec des nattes en bambou tressé et chacun des participants avait à disposition un petit lit de camp pliable et une chaise de la dynastie chinoise Ming ou Qing. Le projet peut être interprété comme une expérience sociale dont le but est d'altérer la perception, développer la prise de conscience et diffuser des informations. L'éclairage de l'individu est un thème qui se répète dans toutes les œuvres d'art et d'architecture de Ai Weiwei.

Come parte dell'opera d'arte "Fairytale 1001" per documenta 12, Ai Weiwei inviò nell'estate del 2007, 1001 cittadini cinesi a Kassel, in Germania. Per ospitarli, adattò a dormitorio gli spazi di una fabbrica di tende installando un sistema di pareti divisorie sospese. Utilizzando un sistema di leggeri telai in acciaio in combinazione con tende in tessuto, creò delle zone riservate sia per dormire che come spogliatoi. Sul pavimento vennero stese delle stuoie in bambù intrecciato e per ogni partecipante furono messe a disposizione una brandina pieghevole e una sedia della dinastia Cinese Ming o Qing. Il progetto può essere inteso come esperimento sociale che ha come scopo quello di alterare la percezione, sviluppare la presa di coscienza e divulgare informazioni. L' illuminazione dell'individuo è un tema che si ripete in tutte le opere d'arte e architettoniche di Ai Weiwei.

"童话1001宿舍" 作为艾未未第12届"文献展"的献展作品"童话1001"的一部分，他在2007年夏天向德国卡塞尔派去了1001名中国人。为了给这些人提供住所，他将一个帐篷工厂改为宿舍。改造工作通过安装悬吊式分隔系统完成。他使用轻型钢结构结合布窗帘，提供睡觉和换衣服的私人空间。地板上铺上竹子编成的席子，每个参与者的位置旁边都放着可折叠的帆布床，并与明清时代的椅子相结合。该项工程可以看成是一项社会实验，目的在于改变理解，提高认识，传播信息。对于个人的启蒙则是贯穿于他的艺术作品与建筑的主题。

INSTALLATION
VENICE BIENNIAL
VENICE, ITALY
Cooperation with Herzog & de Meuron
Design date: 2008

INDEX

AI WEIWEI
FAKE DESIGN
258 Caochangdi Chaoyang District
Beijing 100015, China
Tel. +86 10 8456 4194
Fax + 86 10 8456 4194
aiweiwei.architecture@gmail.com

Ai Weiwei

Born 1957 in Beijing, China, lives and works in Beijing, China.
In the same year of his birth, due to an anti-intellectual campaign, his father Ai Qing – one of the best-known contemporary poets – was sent to Xinjiang, northeast China together with the whole family. In 1978 the family was allowed to return to Beijing and Ai Weiwei enrolled at the Beijing Film Institute. Together with other young artists he formed the Stars Group in Beijing in 1979. In 1981 he moved to New York where he studied at the Parsons School of Design. He returned to Beijing in 1993. In the following years he was editor for different influential art books. In the same period he was cofounder of the China Art Archives and Warehouse. In 1999 he moved to Caochangdi where he started his architectural office FAKE Design in 2003. FAKE Design developed many architectural projects in different parts of China. Ai Weiwei also had consulting cooperations with Swiss offices like Herzog & de Meuron and HHF architects. His architectural projects range from furniture, interior, architecture to landscape design and urban tactics.

Most Recent Solo Exhibitions

2010	Dropping the Urn, ceramics 5000 BCE - 2010 CE, Arcadia University Gallery, Glenside, USA
	The Unilever Series: Ai Weiwei, Turbine Hall, Tate Modern, London, UK
	Ai Weiwei, Galerie Urs Meile, Lucerne, Switzerland
	Barely something, Stiftung DKM, Duisburg, Germany
2009	With Milk, Mies van der Rohe Pavilion, Barcelona, Spain
	World Map, Faurschou Gallery, Beijing, China
	So sorry, Haus der Kunst, Munich, Germany
	According to What?, Mori Art Museum, Tokyo, Japan
	Ways Beyond Art, Ivory Press Space, Madrid, Spain
	Ai Weiwei: New York Photographs 1983-1993, Three Shadows Photography Art Centre, Beijing, China
2008	Ai Weiwei, Albion Gallery, London, UK
	Ai Weiwei, Hyundai Gallery, Seoul, Korea
	Under Construction, Sherman Contemporary Art Foundation, Campbelltown Arts Center, Sydney, Australia
	Illumination, Mary Boone Gallery, New York, USA
	Go China! Ai Weiwei, Groninger Museum, Groningen, The Netherlands

Selected Architectural Group Exhibitions

2010	Contemplating the Void, Guggenheim Museum, New York, USA
	Biennale di Architettura, 12th International Architecture Exhibition, Venice, Italy
	Taking a Stance, 8 Critical Attitudes in Chinese and Dutch Architecture and Design, Today Art Museum, Beijing and Dutch Culture Center, Shanghai, China
2008	Out there: Architecture Beyond Building, Biennale di Architettura, 11th International Architecture Exhibition, Venice, Italy Cooperation with Herzog & de Meuron
2006	Detours. Tactical Approaches to Urbanization in China, Eric Arthur Gallery, Faculty of Architecture, Landscape and Design, University of Toronto, Canada
	Herzog & de Meuron. No 250. Eine Ausstellung, Haus der Kunst, Munich, Germany
	CHINA contemporary. Architecture, Art and Visual Culture, Netherlands Architecture Institute, Rotterdam, The Netherlands
2005	Herzog & de Meuron. An Exhibition, Tate Modern, London, UK
	No 250. An Exhibition. Beauty and Waste in the Architecture of Herzog & de Meuron, Netherlands Architecture Institute, Rotterdam, The Netherlands
2004	Biennale di Architettura, 9th International Architecture Exhibition, Venice, Italy
	Herzog & de Meuron. No 250. Eine Ausstellung, Schaulager, Basel, Switzerland
2001	Tu Mu. Young Chinese Architecture, Aedes Galerie, Berlin, Germany

Work list

2009   Jiading Malu, Shanghai, China

211 Caochangdi, Caochangdi, Beijing, China

2008   Urban planning and landscape design of Ordos 100, Ordos, Inner Mongolia, China

Interior renovation of Alexander Ochs Gallery, Berlin, Germany

The Great Pyramid, Dessau, Germany

The Dog House, Tokyo, Japan

Installation, in cooperation with Herzog & de Meuron at Biennale di Venezia, Italy

2007   Undercover Villa, Ordos, Inner Mongolia, China

Kerry Center Auction House, Beijing, China

Artfarm, in cooperation with HHF, New York, USA

Jiangnanhui, Hangzhou, Zhejiang, China

Fairytale dormitory: temporary interior installation for the project "Fairytale 1001" at documenta 12, Kassel, Germany

241 Caochangdi, Caochangdi, Beijing, China

Red Brick Art Galleries, Caochangdi, Beijing, China

Kunming Art Valley, Kunming, Yunnan, China

Naga Interior Design, in cooperation with EXH, Beijing, China

Lage Restaurant, Shanghai, China

2006   Tsai Residence, in cooperation with HHF, New York, USA

Three Shadows Photography Art Center, Caochangdi, Beijing, China

Shulang Factory, Yantai, Shandong, China

2005   Qingdao Creative Media Institute of Beijing Film Academy, in cooperation with Herzog & de Meuron, Qingdao, Shandong, China

Tree House, in cooperation with HHF, Lijiang, Yunnan, China

Landscape design of Jinhua Architectural Art Park, Jinhua, Zhejiang, China

Cola House, Hangzhou, Zhejiang, China

Bian Bian shopping street, Jiuzhaigou, Sichuan, China

Clubhouse of Water Villa, Lijiang, Yunnan, China

Huan Bi Tang Gallery: interior design, Beijing, China

Memorial for mountain climbers, Huangshan, Anhui, China

Courtyard 104 - Urs Meile Gallery, Caochangdi, Beijing, China

2004   Space design of Ya Bar, Beijing, China

Courtyard 105, Caochangdi, Beijing, China

Neolithic Pottery Museum, Jinhua Architectural Art Park, Jinhua, Zhejiang, China

Landscape design of Beijing's 2008 Olympics, Beijing, China

National Stadium for Beijing's 2008 Olympics in cooperation with Herzog & de Meuron, Beijing, China

Nine Boxes, Beijing, China

Cuo House, Beijing, China

Six Rooms, Nanjing, Jiangsu, China

Go Where Restaurant, Beijing, China

2003   Landscape design of Ai Qing Middle School, Jinhua, Zhejiang, China

Commercial & Cultural Center of Jingdong New District, in cooperation with Herzog & de Meuron, Jinhua, Zhejiang, China

Songshan Lake Culture and Exhibition Center, Dongguan, Guangdong, China

2002   Landscape design of Yiwu river bank, Jinhua, Zhejiang, China

Landscape design of Ai Qing Cultural Park, Jinhua, Zhejiang, China

University of Visual Art, Shanghai, China

Anter Automotive Factory, Huaiyin, Jiangsu, China

2001   Landscape design of Commune by The Great Wall, Beijing, China

Boao Villa, Haikou, Hainan, China

Bar Jia 55, Beijing, China

2000   Landscape design of Soho Contemporary City, Beijing, China

In Between: installation, Beijing, China

China Art Archives and Warehouse, Caochangdi, Beijing, China

1999   Ai Weiwei Studio, Caochangdi, Beijing, China

Publications

- Ai Weiwei – Herzog & de Meuron, Beijing, Venice, London (2008) (Catalogue). London: Albion Gallery.
- Koegel, Eduard (2007). Ai Weiwei. Fake Design in the Village (Catalogue). Berlin: Aedes.

Selected bibliography

- Ai Weiwei (2009). Sichuan Earthquake. In: Ai Weiwei, Andrew Mackenzie, Joseph Grima (authors). 10 x 10 / 3.100 Architects, 10 Critics. London, New York: Phaidon Press Ltd. p. 418.
- Adam, Hubertus (2007). Follies am Flussufer. Jinhua Architectural Park, 2004–2006. In: Archithese, 08.08.2007. p. 40.
- Adam, Hubertus (2009). Mehr Wandfläche, bitte! In: Bauwelt, 15/09, 17. April 2009. pp. 32–37.
- Ai Weiwei (2008). Warum das Nationalstadion dem Volk gehören muss. In: Bauwelt, No.29/30 2008. pp.18–25.
- Ai Weiwei; Herzog, Jacques (2007). Concept and Fake. In: Parkett, 81. pp.122–132.
- Ai Weiwei; Herzog, Jacques (2008). Concept and Fake. In: Ai Weiwei – Herzog & de Meuron, Beijing, Venice, London (catalogue, Volume 1). London: Albion Gallery. pp.111–122.
- Ai Weiwei; Herzog, Jacques (2008). The "Bird's Nest" will be better used after the Olympics. In: Beijing Today, issue 28/2008. pp. 26–29.
- Arruda, Tereza de (2009): China. Construction – Deconstruction (catalogue). Sao Paolo: Museu de Arte de Sao Paolo; Beijing: Chinablue Gallery.
- Bernstein, Fred A. (2008). In Inner Mongolia. Pushing Architecture'e Outer Limits. www.nytimes.com/2008/05/01/garden/01mongolia.html?sq=ai%20weiwei&st=cse&scp=18&pagewanted=all
- Betsky, Aaron (2008). Eating One's Bird's Nest and Having It Too: Ai Weiwei Photographs the National Stadium, Beijing. In: Ai Weiwei & Herzog & de Meuron, Beijing, Venice, London (catalogue, Volume 1). London: Albion Gallery pp.105–109.
- Chen Shuyu (2006). Fast City, Instant Landscape: Seventeen Urban Public Mini-structures in Jinhua Architecture Park, Zhejiang. In: Time+Architecture, 1/2006. pp. 42–45.
- Flora Zhang (2008). China's Olympic Crossroads. Bird's nest designer Ai Weiwei on Beijing's Pretend Smile.
- Greco, Claudio (2008). The 'revolution' of Caochangdi. In: The Skira Yearbook of World Architecture 2007–2008 (Francesco, Jodice; Molinari, Luca; Eds). Milano: Skira Editore. pp.140–141.
- Greco, Claudio; Santoro, Carlo (2007). Beijing. The new city. Milano: Skira Editore.
- Haduch, Bartosz; Haduch, Michał (2008). Zielone miasto. In: Architektura & Biznes, 09/2008. pp. 60–69.
- Hart, Sara (2004). 2008 Beijing Olympics. Innovative Architecture ready to change the Face on an Ancient City. In: Architectural Records, 3. pp. 100–105.
- Hosch, Alexander (2007). China's Renaissance Man. In: Architectural Digest, March 2007. pp. 44–49, 204.
- Jodidio, Philip (2007). Fake Design. In: Architecture in China. Cologne: Taschen. pp. 61–66.
- Jodidio, Philip (2009). Ai Weiwei – Fake Design. In: Architecture Now 6. Cologne: Taschen. pp. 72–75.
- Klein, Caroline; Vlassenrood, Linda (2006). In: CHINA Contemporary. Architecture, Art, Visual Culture (Catalogue) Rotterdam: NAi Publishers. pp. 186–187, 352–353.
- Klein, Caroline; Kögel, Eduard (2005). Made in China. Neue chinesische Architektur. München: DVA. pp. 22–29.
- Koegel, Eduard (2008). 104 Courtyard, Urs Meile Gallery Ateliers and Exhibition Space. In: Domez, 72, September 2008. pp. 142–149.
- Koegel, Eduard (2008). 105 Courtyard renovation. In: Domez, 72, September 2008. pp.150–157.
- Kreuger, Justus (2006). Soul Reversal. In: Perspective, October 2006. pp.116–120.
- Liu Qing (2009). Interview with Ai Weiwei. In: Urban Environment Design (Chinese), no. 32, May 2009, p.156–157.
- Lorenz, Andreas (2009). Stadtbau in China. Brüllender Architekturzoo. Manager-Magazin, 09.04.2009. www.manager-magazin.de/life/wohnen/0,2828,617172,00.html

- Lu Heng-Zhong (2006). An Interview with Ai Weiwei, One of the Architects of Jinhua Architecture Park, Zhejiang In: Time + Architecture, 1. pp. 46 – 65.

- Merewether, Charles (2008).Beijing, Venice, London. In: Ai Weiwei & Herzog & de Meuron, Beijing, Venice, London (catalogue, Volume 2). London: Albion Gallery. pp. 87 – 111.

- Mingels, Guido (2007). Ein Nest für das neue China. In: Das Magazin, 15. pp. 24 – 37.

- Mingels, Guido (2007). Pekings Olympiastadion – Vorzeigearchitektur für eine Diktatur und die Frage an deren Schweizer Schöpfer: Darf man das bauen? Vogelnest und Kuckucksei. In: Der Tagesspiegel, 19630. p. 3.

- Muynck, Bert de (2009). Ordos 100. In: Perspective Plus, Architecture + Construction Yearbook 2009. Hong Kong: Perspective Limited. pp. 110 – 121.

- Muynck, Bert de (2009). Babel for Billionaires. In: Mark, No.15, August/September 2008. pp.124 – 135.

- Pearman, Hugh (2004). Iconoclasm rules: How Herzog & de Meuron work with conceptual artist Ai Weiwei on Beijing's new Olympic stadium.
www.artnet.de/magazine/features/herold/herold07-20-07.asp
http://hughpearman.com/articles5/weiwei.html

- Péus, Camilla (2007). Kunstkaiser. In: Architektur und Wohnen, 3. pp. 111 – 120.

- Poncellini, Luca (2008). Ai Weiwei's controversity. In: The Skira Yearbook of World Architecture 2007 – 2008 (Francesco, Jodice; Molinari, Luca). Milano: Skira Editore. pp.142 – 143.

- Young, Michael (2009). All Dogs go to Heaven. Tokyo's flamboyant art patron Johnnie Walker, aka Joni Waka, commissions Ai Weiwei to memorialize his beloved dog in a new building. In: Art Asia Pacific 64, Jul-Aug 2009. pp. 66 – 67.

HHF architects

www.hhf.ch
HHF architects was founded 2003 in Basel, Switzerland by Tilo Herlach, Simon Hartmann and Simon Frommenwiler. Since then HHF architects realised and worked on several projects in Switzerland, China, USA, Germany, Italy and Mexico. An important constituent of the office is teaching at universities such as: ETH Studio Basel, EPFL Lausanne, MIT Boston and UIA Mexico.

Herzog & de Meuron

Jacques Herzog and Pierre de Meuron established their office in Basel in 1978. Currently the practice employs 340 collaborators working on nearly 40 projects across Europe, North and South America and Asia. The firm's head office is in Basel with branch offices in Hamburg, London, Madrid and New York. Since 1994 Jacques Herzog and Pierre de Meuron are visiting professors at Harvard University, and professors at ETH Zurich since 1999, where they co-founded the ETH Studio Basel - Contemporary City Institute in 2002. Herzog & de Meuron have been awarded numerous prizes including the Pritzker Architecture Prize in 2001. Their work has appeared in numerous publications and exhibitions worldwide.

Photocredits

Ai Weiwei – Fake Design
Iwan Baan
Herzog & de Meuron
HHF

Many thanks to

Ai Weiwei
Fake Design Team
Herzog & de Meuron
HHF

Published and distributed worldwide by
DAAB MEDIA GMBH
Maastrichter Str. 53
50672 Cologne / Germany
tel. + 49 221 690 48 210
fax + 49 221 690 48 229
www.daab-media.com

Join our community
www.edaab.com
and present your work to a worldwide audience

Printed in Italy

ISBN 978-3-942597-01-2

Edited by Caroline Klein

Caroline Klein studied Interior Design in Florence and
Architecture at the Technical University of Munich. She
has been working for different renowned architectural
offices as well as a freelance writer, producer and editor
for international architectural magazines and publishers.

Concept by Ralf Daab
Creative director: Feyyaz
Layout by Sonia Mion, Nicola Iannibello
www.ventizeronove.it

Introduction by Caroline Klein

Chinese translation by Sinonet, Kann Yujing
French translation by Emmanuel Gallina
German translation by Caroline Klein
Italian translation by Diana D'Anselmo
Spanish translation by Silvia La Sala

Copy editing by Caroline Klein
English copy editing by Jacky Choo

Litho fgv GROUP, Milan
www.fgvgrafica.it